"Kiel has produced a tremendous
sources, both ancient and modern
justice. With unexpected but poin
Catholic social teaching for people today, he challenges readers to consider
how this teaching might transform their lives and the world."

— Julia H. Brumbaugh, associate professor of religious studies,
    Regis University (Colorado)

"A hallmark of the much-needed renewal of Roman Catholic moral
theology has been the restoration of the word of God to a central place
in its reflection. In this highly readable work, Micah Kiel invites us to
a lifelong adventure that is provoked by the person of Christ and the
message of the gospels. Though such a journey is demanding and usually
rejected by worldly hearts, the humble and persevering pilgrim will know
the joyful experience of following the Teacher home."

— Cardinal Joseph Tobin, CSsR

"If you were to ask a scripture scholar, a storyteller, a teacher, and a faithful
Catholic how we are called to live as disciples of Christ, this book is the
energetic and hopeful response. Kiel's profoundly pragmatic chapters
fluidly connect resources and ruminations from Scripture and Catholic
social thought to lead us to consider how to respond with generosity
to everyday dilemmas. I found myself drawn in and humbled by his
vulnerable personal revelations about his failings, which we all share
because (as he emphasizes) we are people bound together on life's journey
seeking to live more justly. His deep and intuitive grasp of both Hebrew
and Christian texts roots more current expressions of community, such as
common good and social sin, making clear that God's revelation has always
called us to live for and with others as a Eucharistic people."

— Alison M. Benders, emerita, Jesuit School of Theology,
    Santa Clara University, and author of Just Prayer

Be Transformed

A Biblical Journey toward a More Just World

Micah D. Kiel

LITURGICAL PRESS
Collegeville, Minnesota

litpress.org

Cover art: *Glitch Transfiguration* (front) and *The Transfiguration* (back), Kelly Latimore, kellylatimoreicons.com. Used with permission.

Scripture quotations are from New Revised Standard Version Bible: Catholic Edition © 1989, 1993 National Council of the Churches of Christ in the United States of America. Used by permission. All rights reserved worldwide.

Library of Congress Cataloging-in-Publication Data

Names: Kiel, Micah D., author.
Title: Be transformed : a biblical journey toward a more just world / Micah D. Kiel.
Description: Collegeville, Minnesota : Liturgical Press, [2024] | Includes index. | Summary: "Be Transformed brings together Catholic Social Teaching and Scripture and applies them to instances of injustice in our world today. When understood together, Catholic Social Teaching and Scripture will profile authentically Christian ways to live in a world dominated by greed, division, environmental destruction, and violence. Be Transformed will deepen our understanding and challenge readers to consult these traditions when making life decisions"— Provided by publisher.
Identifiers: LCCN 2024017222 (print) | LCCN 2024017223 (ebook) | ISBN 9798400800207 (trade paperback) | ISBN 9798400800214 (epub) | ISBN 9798400800221 (pdf)
Subjects: LCSH: Social justice—Religious aspects—Catholic Church. | Christian sociology—Catholic Church.
Classification: LCC BX1795.S62 K44 2024 (print) | LCC BX1795.S62 (ebook) | DDC 261.8—dc23/eng/20240605
LC record available at https://lccn.loc.gov/2024017222
LC ebook record available at https://lccn.loc.gov/2024017223

For my students
past, present, and future

Contents

Preface

The very first tear he made was so deep that I thought it had gone right into my heart. And when he began pulling the skin off, it hurt worse than anything I've ever felt. The only thing that made me able to bear it was just the pleasure of feeling the stuff peel off.[1]

These words are spoken by Eustace Clarence Scrubb, the unfortunate, selfish, and recalcitrant main character of C. S. Lewis's *Voyage of the Dawn Treader*. Greed had turned Eustace into a dragon. Only Aslan can save him by ripping away his old self and setting him on his human feet anew.

The uncomfortable image of flesh being ripped away is appropriate for the topics in this book. An authentically Christian life should result in us becoming a new creation: "everything old has passed away; see, everything has become new!" (2 Cor 5:17). But what does it mean to be a new creation? What does an authentically Christian life look like? These types of questions, and many more, will be addressed in the pages of this book. By close examination of the Bible and Catholic social teaching we will find a deep challenge and burden: we are called to a personal transformation that also transforms the world. If we meet the challenge, our old selves—both personally and as a society—will need to be cast aside.

I owe thanks and gratitude to many who have helped me complete this project. As always, I receive support and encouragement from my colleagues in the theology department at St. Ambrose University. I am grateful for receiving a sabbatical in the fall of 2022. I also received

---

1. C. S. Lewis, *Voyage of the Dawn Treader* (New York: Harper Trophy, 1952).

grant funding from the Faculty Development Committee and the Baecke Endowment for the Humanities at St. Ambrose to support travel and research in Turkey and Greece. St. Ambrose has been, and continues to be, a wonderful place for me to live out my vocation as a teacher and scholar.

I also am indebted to my family, who regularly endure my theological rants and are often the first sounding board for my ideas, whether at family dinner or on the way home from Sunday Mass. I treasure our family adventures more than anything else in my life. My wife Eleanor continues to be my first, and most insightful, reader.

My friends Ken Novak and Sarah Adams graciously read and commented on the entire manuscript. They gave me invaluable insights and pushed my thinking in important ways. Thanks, also, to Hailey Cox and Katiane Rivera for their excellent help. At a few points they've graciously allowed me to use their ideas. I'm ultimately responsible for all this, of course.

In 1998–1999 I was a volunteer teacher in Benque Viejo del Carmen, a small town on the Guatemalan border in western Belize. I just recently returned there, with my family in tow, for the first time in twenty-five years. When I think about the content of this book, much of it can trace its origins to that year. My students opened to me their lives and their hearts. The firsthand experience with a kind of poverty I had never seen before prodded me to ask questions and rethink what it means to have a life of faith. These questions continue in my volunteer work at the Café on Vine, where we serve meals to the hungry and homeless in Davenport. I am grateful to Waunita Sullivan for inviting me into this community and especially for our daily guests there, who radiate the real presence of Christ.

During the 2024 spring semester, I interviewed, was offered, and accepted a position at St. John's University and School of Theology and the College of St. Benedict. This marks a return to my alma mater, a place that has always felt like home to my wife and me. I am very grateful to Shawn Colberg, Kristin Colberg, and Kari-Shane Davis Zimmerman, and many other new colleagues at CSB+SJU. I am excited about the next chapter of my life and vocation in the Benedictine tradition.

The secret joy of being a teacher is that we learn as much as, if not more than, our students do. My ninth-grade math students in Belize, the thousands of undergraduates at St. Ambrose, and the many deacon candidates and their wives whom I have taught are a through line in my life and work. This book would not have been possible without the conversations and relationships I have had with them across the years. I dedicate this book to my students.

Micah D. Kiel
Feast of the Conversion of St. Paul
Davenport, IA

Abbreviations

CA   *Centesimus Annus*

CCC   *Catechism of the Catholic Church*

CSDC   *Compendium of the Social Doctrine of the Church*

CV   *Caritas in Veritate*

EE   *Ecclesia de Eucharistia*

EG   *Evangelii Gaudium*

GS   *Gaudium et Spes*

LS   *Laudato Si'*

MM   *Mater et Magistra*

PP   *Populorum Progressio*

PT   *Pacem in Terris*

QA   *Quadragesimo Anno*

RN   *Rerum Novarum*

SC   *Sacramentum Caritatis*

SRS   *Solicitudo Rei Socialis*

Introduction

Be Metamorphosized

Johnny Cash made me write this book.

> Come heed me, my brothers, come heed, one and all
> Don't brag about standing or you'll surely fall
> You're shining your light and shine it you should
> But you're so heavenly minded, you're no earthly good.
>
> If you're holding heaven, then spread it around
> There's hungry hands reaching up here from the ground
> Move over and share the high ground where you stood
> So heavenly minded, you're no earthly good.

From the moment Jesus first appeared in Galilee, a primary temptation for his followers has been to stare upward, concerned only with our eternal destiny. After Jesus' ascension, angels admonish the first disciples for craning their necks upward: "Men of Galilee, why do you stand looking up toward heaven?" (Acts 1:11). If we become too heavenly minded, we will be no earthly good.

Many Catholics today think that their faith is an individual thing, as if our job is nothing more than to get to heaven. Such an understanding of faith, however, is not fully Christian. A faith that only cares about heaven ignores deep biblical truths and clear teachings from the church that Christian faith is about both our own personal salvation *and* our responsibility to make the world a better place.

As members of the human family and citizens of planet earth, the world's problems are our problems. The church teaches us that we have a grave responsibility to change the world and to care about the plight of all God's creatures. In order to live an authentically Christian life, the saving grace we experience from God should compel us to look to do the same for others. We need to ask: "Am I okay with the world around me?" "Where can I help?" "What can we do?" "How can I love my neighbor?"

Any authentic attempt to provide earthly good, while honored by God, will be hated by humans. Living a truly Christlike life rarely ends with the rustic pastoral scenes that people envision as the good life. On the contrary, as was the case for Jesus himself, those who live the faith most authentically often face rejection, ridicule, or worse. The world humans create for themselves—built on greed and accumulation—looks nothing like the world that God wants. God wants justice in the social realm, and when confronted with God's vision, humans will shut it down. We do not lack, however, examples from Christian history of brave individuals who have lived such a life.

Metamorphosis

In the year 1209, Francis of Assisi traveled to Rome. He had a small band of followers who were living an austere life together in Umbria. Francis had written a set of rules for these followers, for which he sought papal approval. But he was worried. A life of poverty, austerity, and itinerant preaching did not seem in step with the church's marble halls and the spires of Gothic cathedrals popping up all over Europe. Francis ultimately succeeded because his core argument was simple, accurate, and persuasive: The Christian life calls everyone to live with simplicity, seeking peace and balance with the surrounding world. Pope Innocent, ruling from the hulking walls of St. John Lateran, the Cathedral Church of Rome, could not miss the authenticity in Francis's message. The Gospel—the core content of what the church preaches and teaches from Scripture and tradition—requires radical living. Francis sought to change the world by convincing people to live in a new way, renouncing wealth and power and living instead with simplicity and sacrifice.

Francis's life offers an example of profound change and conversion. He renounced the wealth into which he was born, a shock to his family of ascendant merchants. Every Christian today is called to this same type of conversion. Scripture is replete with similar examples of a midlife U-turn—some instantaneous, some gradual. Moses becomes God's prophet after talking with a burning bush; Peter and the disciples dropped their nets and followed Jesus; Paul went from persecuting the church to being its strongest advocate; and Mary's assent to God's plan for her life changed her own future and that of humanity. While we today may not hear God's voice audibly speaking to us like Francis did, the call for transformation and conversion is no less clear.

The title for this book, "Be Transformed," is taken from Paul's letter to the Romans. Paul ends his longest missive by profiling what an authentically Christian life should look like. The goal of every Christian life is to be transformed:

> I appeal to you therefore, brothers and sisters, by the mercies of God, to present your bodies as a living sacrifice, holy and acceptable to God, which is your spiritual worship. Do not be conformed to this world, but *be transformed* by the renewing of your minds, so that you may discern what is the will of God—what is good and acceptable and perfect. (Rom 12:1-2; italics added)

The Greek word translated here as "transformation" is *metamorphosis.* It's a dramatic word, literally meaning to change into a different form. For example, there's a famous ancient novel by Apuleius called the *Metamorphosis*, in which the main character is turned into a donkey.

While he wasn't changed into a donkey, Jesus himself undergoes a profound metamorphosis, which is the word Matthew and Mark use to narrate what we traditionally call the transfiguration (Matt 17:1-7; Mark 9:2-8). Jesus takes Peter, James, and John up a mountain, where he is "metamorphized" before them. Jesus' clothes become dazzling white and his face is "like the sun" (Matt 17:2). He chats with Elijah and Moses. Jesus' transformation is so dramatic that the disciples are afraid and "did not know what to say" (Mark 9:6). Metamorphosis is a dramatic change; it allows for no half measures. The word signifies a complete transformation.

The only other use of the word *metamorphosis* in the Bible comes from one of Paul's letters:

> And all of us, with unveiled faces, seeing the glory of the Lord as though reflected in a mirror, are being transformed into the same image from one degree of glory to another; for this comes from the Lord, the Spirit. (2 Cor 3:18)

When Paul says that we are "being transformed" into the image of God, he suggests that transformation is ongoing. While there are examples from Scripture and tradition of immediate transformation (think of Paul on the road to Damascus), being transformed more and more into the image of Christ is a lifelong evolution.

What does Paul mean when he says we should be metamorphosized? What does transformation look like in practical terms? He continues in Romans 12 with many details of what a transformed life looks like:

- Do not think of yourself more highly than you ought to (v. 3)
- Let love be genuine (v. 9)
- Extend hospitality to strangers (v. 13)
- Bless, and do not curse, those who persecute you (v. 14)
- Live in harmony with one another (v. 16)
- Do not be haughty (v. 16)
- Associate with the lowly (v. 16)
- Do not repay evil with evil (v. 17)
- Live peaceably with all (v. 18)

Paul's profile of a transformed life is focused on relationships. The metamorphosis he describes is not a spiritual one, but an interpersonal one. To be sure, his call to live in peace, harmony, and love is founded upon and made possible by spiritual realities (as the first eight chapters of Romans makes clear). But the implication of our spiritual salvation must always be evident in present realities such as relationships, communities, and societies.

Paul's list describing a transformed life might seem daunting. Accomplishing even one of these practices in a lifetime would be difficult, let alone all of them. Part of the difficulty lies in the fact that our world opposes a transformed life at every turn. The way of our world is a path of least resistance. The well-worn tracks of selfishness, greed, accumulation, retribution, and self-promotion are so ingrained that we do not even recognize them as patterns of behavior, much less see the path for an alternative.

Scripture and Catholic Social Teaching

This book has one simple goal: to prod Christians, and in particular comfortable Roman Catholics, to think about the way in which their faith compels them to care about others and not just themselves. I mean something more than having a vague sense of angst at the suffering of others. We need to do more than just send money to the Red Cross when there's a natural disaster or put change into our Lenten rice bowl. Our Christian faith calls for a metamorphosis into self-sacrificial living for others. We must seek, in every moment and encounter, the good of the other, not our own. To live this way requires a process of lifelong transformation, leaving behind "an individualistic, indifferent and self-centered mentality" and replacing it with one that is "humane, noble and fruitful" (EG 208).[1] To accomplish this goal, I will turn to two bodies of literature: Scripture and Catholic social teaching.

Most Catholics are generally aware of Scripture, perhaps specifically with what we might call the "holy trinity" of justice texts:

> But let justice roll down like waters,
> and righteousness like an ever-flowing stream. (Amos 5:24)

> "He has told you, O mortal, what is good;
>   and what does the LORD require of you
> but to do justice, and to love kindness,
>   and to walk humbly with your God?" (Mic 6:8)

> "Truly I tell you, just as you did it to one of the least of these . . .
> you did it to me." (Matt 25:40)

---

1. Pope Francis, *Evangelii Gaudium*, Apostolic Exhortation on the Proclamation of the Gospel in Today's World, November 24, 2013, https://www.vatican.va/content /francesco/en/apost_exhortations/documents/papa-francesco_esortazione-ap_2013 1124_evangelii-gaudium.html.

These texts are obviously important, but they also barely scratch the surface of what Scripture says about living a transformed life.

The texts of the Bible, written across almost a thousand years, come to us from a distant time and place. Although ancient, they challenge humanity's sinful ways and present timeless critiques of our structures of exclusion. In the chapters that follow we will examine all the hidden corners of the Bible that can help us deepen our understanding of what God wants from us and for our world. The Old Testament is replete with laws and regulations that make provision for the disadvantaged. Many prophetic texts call for the rich to make a just society for the poor and the marginalized. In the New Testament, Jesus' own self-sacrifice provides a model for all Christians. Paul's image of the body of Christ is one in which the weak are enshrined at the center and empowered.

Our understanding of God's will does not stop with Scripture. The church also offers us moral guidelines through a group of writings known as Catholic social teaching. These texts form a unified yet ever-developing body of teaching from popes and bishops over the last 130 years. They provide sociological and theological analysis of troubling social trends and make comment and judgment upon how Catholics ought to think and respond. Few Catholics are familiar with these teachings. We may be aware of the church's commitment to life or the need for charity, but this leaves much unexplored. The church's social teaching shows us how to emulate God's love for us by applying that love to the world. In these documents, the church evaluates and offers guidance on issues such as poverty, war, the environment, human dignity, inequality, work, and the economy.

God is the source of all revelation, which comes to us in the specific streams of Scripture and tradition. In other words, the Bible and the church's teachings are two of the primary ways God speaks to us today about God's will. These teachings are not only about our own spirituality and salvation, but also relate to society as a whole. God wants our salvation and God wants a just world; in fact, as we will see in the following chapters, these two things are linked. These teachings about social reality come to us in the highest forms of revelation that the church can offer. The Bible, papal encyclicals, and dogmatic constitutions of the church are the most authoritative teachings we have. They come to us not as suggestions but as grave obligations.

One of the things that I hope will make this book unique is the way in which I bring together Scripture and Catholic social teaching.[2] The church's social teaching is built on the foundation of Scripture, but often its use of Scripture is thin and underdeveloped. For example, the prophet Amos, who is a voice for justice within the Bible, is rarely ever referred to in the church's social documents. As another example, the United States Conference of Catholic Bishops has published a "Scripture Guide" as a companion to their teaching on social issues.[3] While the information here is fine, it is just a list of texts that can apply to Catholic social teaching, sort of like putting a series of bumper stickers on the back of a car. It lacks depth.

The church, as I like to say, leaves a lot on the bone when it comes to its use of Scripture. There are depths never reached and details left unexplored. By plumbing these depths and lingering over the details, three things can happen:

1. The way in which Catholic social teaching fits into the Catholic tradition will become more apparent. These documents are sometimes dismissed as not being essential, or not being the core of what the church teaches. Recognizing the biblical depths of our social teaching will help us see the continuity between Scripture and these magisterial documents.

2. Scripture can make Catholic social teaching less boring! Sometimes the church's social teaching is very cerebral—often philosophical

---

2. The scholarly field has plenty of books on the Bible and justice, but few, if any of them, intentionally attempt to bring together Scripture and the social teaching of the church. For example, John R. Donahue, *Seek Justice That You May Live: Reflections and Resources on the Bible and Social Justice* (New York: Paulist Press, 2014), offers a very thorough assessment of biblical texts and justice. This book, however, makes no engagement with the church's social teaching. Another book with a promising title, *Scripture and Social Justice: Catholic and Ecumenical Essays*, ed. Anathea Portier-Young and Gregory E. Sterling (Lanham, MD: Lexington Books/Fortress Press, 2018), also makes no systematic attempt to bring together Scripture and Catholic social teaching together, beyond some sporadic references.

3. United States Conference of Catholic Bishops, "Catholic Social Teaching: Scripture Guide," https://www.usccb.org/beliefs-and-teachings/how-we-teach/catholic-education/campus-ministry/tools-for-action/upload/cst-scripture-guide-donna-update-matt2.pdf.

and sociological—and not gripping or inspiring. The Bible can provide narratives, shouts, and whispers that shake us up and inspire us to live our lives differently. Scripture can give Catholic social teaching an embodiment in the form of real-world examples of what it means to live a transformed life.

3. Bringing together Scripture and Catholic social teaching will push both in new directions. For example, the body of social teaching might allow us to ask new questions—and find new answers— to important modern problems. Take, for example, our modern ecological crisis. This is something that the biblical authors never could have understood in a scientific way. But, if the church's social documents have put it on our radar, then we can explore questions and insights within Scripture that relate to this important topic.

St. Francis had the benefit of hearing God's voice audibly; God spoke to him directly from the San Damiano cross. Although today that may not be the experience of most Catholics, we are not left bereft in discerning God's will for our lives. We have the ability to hear God's voice from Scripture and tradition. The words of Scripture and the church's social teachings come to us as obligations, not as food for thought. When properly understood, these sources challenge the foundations of our lives and our society.

The radical claims within Scripture and Catholic social teaching make themselves easy to push to the sidelines. The lives lived by many Roman Catholics in the Unites States today (including my own) would be challenged and undermined if we were to take these teachings seriously. It's easier to ignore than take seriously our obligation to share our possessions. We listen to a culture that praises accumulation rather than the church's call for solidarity. It's more expedient to align our social goals with a political party than with the church's teaching. Yet these teachings are here for our benefit, and for the world's. As the *Catechism* summarizes: "The Church's social teaching proposes principles for reflection; it provides criteria for judgment; it gives guidelines for action" (CCC 2423).[4]

---

4. *Catechism of the Catholic Church*, 2nd ed. (Washington, DC: United States Catholic Conference, 2000).

Unruly Freedom

While this book seeks to explain and explore the social teachings in Scripture and the church's traditions, it is hard to make these teachings completely practical. Every person's life is different, and thus everyone who reads this book (if anyone does) will have to engage in a path of discernment about what these teachings might mean for her or his life. Everyone's metamorphosis might be unique. An encounter with the word of God is never predictable. Scripture uses the image of a seed to try to get this idea across. The seed grows on its own, without the farmer's help (see Mark 4:26-29). Pope Francis captures this idea in *Evangelii Gaudium* when he writes, "the Church has to accept this unruly freedom of the word, which accomplishes what it will in ways that surpass our calculations and ways of thinking" (EG 22).

While the bulk of the time spent in each of these chapters will focus on concepts and ideas, I will, at the end of each chapter, apply those concepts and ideas to specific situations in our world today. I will discuss prisons, housing, and youth sports—among others—to provide examples of how these teachings can be made practical and concrete. In reality, however, I have no idea where these teachings and concepts might prod Christians to reevaluate their lives. There should rightly be an "unruly freedom" in where the Gospel leads.

In addition, I must make clear that at every turn in this book I should be condemned as a hypocrite. While I work hard to try to make the world a more just place, many aspects of my own life surely exacerbate the problems in our world. I will, at times, use personal stories and anecdotes to help provide illustration of certain ideas. I will also critique aspects of our world in a way that some might find offensive. I never intend to present myself as a paragon of virtue! The ideas and concepts from Scripture and the church's social teaching are just as challenging and condemning of my lifestyle as for anyone else who lives a relatively comfortable, middle-class life in the modern day United States. In fact, in the process of writing this book I have made changes and added encounters to my life. For example, in the midst of writing about our prison system in chapter 1, I decided I needed to learn more and somehow get involved. I trained to be a volunteer with the Seventh Judicial District in Iowa so I can be a mentor to individuals recently released from prison. The relationships I have had through this experience have prodded my own evolution in various ways.

The things I write about in this book are not always easy, and when it comes to the deep teachings of Scripture and Catholic social teaching, I don't pull any punches. These strong words are necessary if Catholics are to rise to the social challenges of our day. I find myself inspired by the words of Kathleen Norris: "A prophet's task is to reveal the fault lines hidden beneath the comfortable surface of the worlds we invent for ourselves . . . the little lies and delusions of control and security that get us through the day."[5] Most of us, me included, spend most of our time ignoring problems and lying to ourselves that it is all okay. Rather than lies and avoidance, what is called for is love. As Pope John Paul II says in *Veritatis Splendor*, "*Jesus asks us to follow him and to imitate him along the path of love, a love which gives itself completely to the brethren out of love for God*: 'This is my commandment, that you love one another as I have loved you'" (VS 20).[6] We know where this journey of love led for Jesus. This path is sacred, although never safe.[7] Where will it lead?

5. Kathleen Norris, *The Cloister Walk* (New York: Riverhead Books, 1997), 3–4.

6. Pope John Paul II, *Veritatis Splendor*, Encyclical Letter on Fundamental Questions of the Church's Moral Teaching, August 6, 1993, https://www.vatican.va /content/john-paul-ii/en/encyclicals/documents/hf_jp-ii_enc_06081993_veritatis -splendor.html.

7. Adapted from a line by C. Clifton Black, "The Face Is Familiar—I Just Can't Place It," in *The Ending of Mark and the Ends of God: Essays in Memory of Donald Harrisville Juel*, ed. Beverly Roberts Gaventa and Patrick D. Miller (Louisville, KY: Westminster/John Knox Press, 2005), 46.

chapter 1

"Be Great!"

Development of Peoples and Human Flourishing

Let this be recorded for a generation to come,
    so that a people yet unborn may praise the LORD:
that he looked down from his holy height,
    from heaven the LORD looked at the earth
to hear the groans of the prisoners,
    to set free those who were doomed to die.

                   —Psalm 102:18-20

At the beginning of Genesis, God tells humanity to "Be fruitful and multiply" (Gen 1:28). We generally think of these words as meaning "Have kids, and lots of them." But the Hebrew words here could also be translated as "Bear fruit and be great." Given that humans have just been created in the image of God, the author likely had much more in mind than just procreation. If we adjust our translation, this verse becomes a call to greatness rather than simply calling for prodigious progeny. We find, then, a command to flourish in all our human situations and abilities. God's first words to humanity tell us to "be great."

A call to "be great" aligns with the overall goal of Catholic social teaching. At its very heart, the social teaching of the church desires that all humans have the freedom, time, and space to flourish. Every human is endowed at birth with a unique vocation, a destiny given by the Creator. The church aims to create the conditions for flourishing by advocating for the "transition from less human conditions to those which are more human" (PP 20).[1]

If the church's teaching sees authentic human development as a goal for all people, we might first stop to ask: why does our world struggle to create such situations? What prevents human flourishing? Why do so many people struggle to "be great"? The answer: Sin. The most recent social encyclicals of the church have started their assessment of society by discussing the problem of sin. Contending with sin is an important starting point in evaluating the problems we face in our world today.

The *Catechism's* first definition of sin says it is a "failure in genuine love for God and neighbor" and that it "injures human solidarity" (CCC 1849). This definition impresses on us two key ideas. First, sin is not just a personal matter; it concerns other people. Second, sin is about more than not doing wrong things. To avoid sin we must live up to our responsibilities: "for what I have done and *what I have failed to do.*" Given these insights, we might define sin as anything that hinders human flourishing. A world without sin is one in which humans can "be great" in the way that God intends.

Sin Two Ways: Individual and Structural/Social

I'm a fan of the actor, writer, and comedian Steve Martin. In one of his lesser-known movies, *Novocaine*, he plays a dentist who makes some bad choices. He has an affair with a patient, who then blackmails him into giving her narcotics as the price for her silence. He ends up killing her. What started as small flirtations and a few bad choices ends with the dentist ensnared in a murder investigation. As his past catches up with him, a police officer asks: "Is it possible you have some peccadilloes that you should tell me about?" (The word "peccadillo" literally means "little sin.") The dentist responds: "Peccadilloes. . . little sins. . . Maybe that's all I was guilty of."

---

1. Pope Paul VI, *Populorum Progressio*, March 26, 1967, in *Catholic Social Thought: Encyclicals and Documents from Pope Leo XIII to Pope Francis*, 3rd ed., ed. David J. O'Brien and Thomas A. Shannon (Maryknoll, NY: Orbis Books, 2016).

We are all guilty of little sins. At the same time, our little sins often snowball, pick up momentum, and get out of control. The church calls this snowballing "structural" or "social" sin. This type of sin takes on a life of its own and infects the society in which we live. Catholic social teaching will ask us to recognize that our peccadilloes, our little sins, can accumulate and be built up into larger structures of sin.

While it makes sense to us intuitively to think about individual sins—person X does something to wrong person Y or Z—we are less likely to think of immense social problems as sinful. Yet this is precisely how the church in its social teaching asks us to think about them. The accumulation of small sins—peccadilloes—is built up into structures of sin that engulf and overcome the people involved. Scripture and tradition give us sin two ways: personal and structural.

Individual Sin and Conversion

Any discussion of sin will start at the beginning, in Eden. The contours here hardly need to be recapitulated; they are the most well-known understanding of sin in the church today. God created a perfect world and Adam and Eve messed it up, thereby passing down a sinful trait to all humans. While we all are faced daily with choices, we are also inherently tainted by this sin that can only be taken away by God's grace and mercy, accessed through Jesus.

The idea of original sin and its relationship to personal responsibility gets its most famous treatment in St. Augustine. In his *Confessions*, he reflects on his own will and choices and how they relate to God:

> What lifted me out into your light was the knowledge that I do have a will; that was as sure as the knowledge that I was alive. It followed that when I wanted or didn't want something, I could be absolutely certain that nothing but myself was doing that wanting or not wanting. And I gradually became aware that in this responsibility lay the cause of my sin.[2]

A doctrine of individual sin posits a straightforward relationship between actor and wrongdoings. We have free will, and we use that

---

2. Augustine, *Confessions*, trans. Sarah Ruden (New York: Modern Library, 2018), 7.2.

free will to make a wrong choice or fail to make a right choice, which results in our sinning. It is this understanding of sin that gives rise to the language in the *Confiteor*, the prayer of confession at Mass: "for what I have done and what I have failed to do."

Conversion

The givenness of our own individual sinfulness reveals the need for conversion. A conversion entails a renewed relationship with God, who changes our hearts of stone into hearts of flesh. The Bible is full of people who have an experience of God—often some sort of radical epiphany—that changes the course of their life. Moses, for example, was confronted with a burning bush and a divine voice proclaiming God's name. Moses' life turns on a dime and he helps liberate God's people (see Exod 1–4). The apostle Paul, who persecuted the church early in his life, found himself blinded by God's brilliance and the course of his life altered (See Acts 9–13 and Gal 1–2).

These scriptural examples of conversion share three things in common. First, they have sin as the backdrop. In Exodus, the people are enslaved and need liberation. In Acts, Paul changes his ways from persecuting the church to promulgating the Gospel. Second, God instigates all of these conversions by irrupting into people's lives. Moses and Paul did not go looking for God, yet God intervened in their lives in a dramatic way.

The third and final commonality of these scriptural examples is that each conversion leads to a new kind of flourishing—an entirely new set of possibilities for life. Conversion did more than change something internally; it set a course for a new way of living. Moses leads the people through the desert to the promised land. Paul starts churches throughout the Mediterranean world. Conversion always goes hand in hand with flourishing.

The word *conversion* comes from a Latin word that means a "turning." Conversion is certainly a turning *away* from sin, but it must also entail a turning *toward* something new. These biblical examples help us see that conversion should turn us towards others and create spaces for authentic human flourishing.

Seeing the examples of Moses and Paul, whose conversions led them to build up a different world, can help us understand why thinking about sin and conversion is so essential for the church's social teaching. If sin is how we explain the problems in our world, then conversion must be part of the solution. The church identifies the same problems in society as social workers, public health advocates, and other fields that work for the positive development of peoples. While such advocates will suggest various social programs and new laws to help the poor, the immigrant, or the environment, the church will always see a different starting point. Pinpointing the original problem as sin allows the entrance of God's grace and mercy for all humans. God's mercy does more than save us individually. As John Paul II says, the "God who is *rich in mercy, the Redeemer of [humanity], the Lord and giver of life*, requires from people clear-cut attitudes which express themselves also in actions or omissions towards one's neighbor" (SRS 36).[3] In other words, there must always be a connection between our own being saved from sin and how that conversion enlivens in us action on behalf of other people. Conversion, for John Paul II, must entail a "change of behavior or mentality or mode of existence," particularly as it pertains to one's neighbor (SRS 38).

In his encyclical about the environment, *Laudato Si'*, Pope Francis invokes John Paul II's use of the word *conversion* in the context of the environmental problems we face in our world. For those who are indifferent, or who think their Christian beliefs do not entail a call to action, what is needed is an ecological conversion, "whereby the effects of their encounter with Jesus Christ become evident in their relationship with the world around them" (LS 217).[4]

It is not an accident that the *Compendium of the Social Doctrine of the Church*, which is a sort of CliffNotes reference guide for the church's social teachings, juxtaposes its discussion of sin with its discussion of humanity's true nature. These two things go hand in hand. Sin is a tragedy that stains both our relationship with God but also with our neighbor and with creation (CSDC 117).[5] At the same time, for

3. Pope John Paul II, *Solicitudo Rei Socialis*, December 30, 1987, in *Catholic Social Thought*, ed. O'Brien and Shannon.

4. Pope Francis, *Laudato Si'*, May 24, 2015, in *Catholic Social Thought*, ed. O'Brien and Shannon.

5. Pontifical Council for Justice and Peace, *Compendium of the Social Doctrine of the Church*, May 26, 2006, https://www.vatican.va/roman_curia/pontifical_councils /justpeace/documents/rc_pc_justpeace_doc_20060526_compendio-dott-soc_en.html.

a human fully to live out her or his calling as a child of God requires a litany of conditions to be properly ordered, including economic, social, juridic, political, and cultural aspects of life (CSDC 137). In other words, turning away from sin is about a lot more than just "not doing bad things." Turning from sin requires a turning toward our neighbor, helping to enable their flourishing. In order to live out God's call to "be great," we must convert to creating the conditions in which all life can flourish.

Structural or Social Sin

While a personal sense of original sin, discussed above, is part of the church's social teaching, it is not the most common paradigm in these writings. Because these documents discuss large social and global issues, sin often gets discussed differently. Evil social realities and structures live in our world. These structures can breed sinful situations, or create injustice, in a way that individual sin alone can't explain. Because of this, the church's social documents frequently talk about "social sin" or "structures of sin."

It might be helpful to begin this discussion with a very mundane example. I recently bought a pack of batteries at Costco. They were encased in such an array of plastic and cardboard that I couldn't open the package without heavy-duty kitchen shears. All of this packaging went to waste. In this type of situation, the church turns to thinking about structures to help explain how and why sin persists in our world.

The *Catechism* defines structural or social sin as the way in which sin is perpetuated through the world that humans have built for themselves. There are ways of being, instituted by humans, that lead people to do wrong (CCC 1869). Did I intentionally commit a sin by buying batteries at Costco? No! That does not mean, however, that there is nothing sinful in participating in a structure that creates such waste. Most examples of structural sin are less trivial than excessive packaging. Immense social problems such as environmental destruction, war, gun violence, or racism can't be explained by simply appealing to individual choices. Something bigger lurks.

The healthcare system in the United States might be another helpful example, and one less trivial than my Costco batteries. Scientific studies reveal that there are significant racial disparities in healthcare outcomes in the United States. We saw this early in the COVID-19 pandemic, when black Americans were more likely to die from infection than white Americans.[6] There are a number of things that explain this fact: lack of access to affordable healthcare; impediments to living a healthy lifestyle; higher rates of smoking and diabetes; and racial bias within local healthcare systems. We should call racial disparity in COVID-19 death rates "sinful." But who is guilty? In such a situation, we can't point a finger at just one person. The whole system is sinful.

When discussing structural sin, my students are always quick to point out the problem of culpability: "Does this mean we're not responsible for the wrong things that we do?" This perceptive question cannot get us off the hook, because structural sins always grow out of and are related to individual sins. John Paul II attempts to explain this dynamic. Despite the reality of structural sin, such sins are "always linked to the concrete acts of individuals who introduce these structures, consolidate them and make them difficult to remove. And thus they grow stronger, spread, and become the source of other sins, and so influence people's behavior" (SRS 36). Individual sins, he continues, give rise to "social institutions that are contrary to divine goodness."

Benedict XVI also uses the language of structures of sin to help explain the predicaments of injustice in our world today. He affirms, of course, the reality of original sin. But he then moves on to discuss how the church's wisdom has "always pointed to the presence of original sin in social conditions and in the structures of society" (CV 34).[7] He uses the economy as an example. An economy that has been left to itself with the assumption that it will work for the betterment of all people and that it should be shielded from questions of a moral nature has led to "economic, social and political systems that trample upon personal and social freedom" (CV 34). In other words, centuries of human economic action motivated only by greed and personal gain have resulted in economic structures that are sinful.

6. "Why Are Blacks Dying at Higher Rates from COVID-19?," *Brookings Institution*, April 9, 2020, https://www.brookings.edu/blog/fixgov/2020/04/09/why-are-blacks-dying-at-higher-rates-from-covid-19/.

7. Pope Benedict XVI, *Caritas in Veritate*, June 29, 2009, in *Catholic Social Thought*, ed. O'Brien and Shannon.

John Paul II says that categories of sin and structures of sin are "seldom applied to the situation of the contemporary world." However, he continues, "one cannot easily gain a profound understanding of the reality that confronts us unless we give a name to the root of the evils which afflict us" (SRS 36). By employing language of the "structures of sin," we are better able to diagnose the problems that face humanity. Our problems are bigger than individual choices. Governments, corporations, societies, and other groups can perpetuate sin. When decisions are made in such a context, determining factors that seem innocuous and based on economics, ideology, class, or technology may actually show their true nature to be sinful.

Ultimately, talking about structures of sin is important because, as John Paul II concludes, we need to understand "the true *nature* of the evil which faces us with respect to the development of peoples: it is a question of a *moral evil*, the fruit of *many sins* which lead to 'structures of sin.' To diagnose the evil in this way is to identify precisely, on the level of human conduct, *the path to be followed* in order *to overcome it*" (SRS 37). John Paul's true concern here is the "development of peoples," showing the importance of human flourishing. Authentic human development is the ability to live one's life freely and to flourish as God intends. When structures squash this ability, constraining our ability to "be great," we must call the situation sinful.

Structural Sin in Amos

For those who are skeptical about the idea of structural sin, it might be helpful to point out how explicit the idea is within Scripture. It amazes me that the church's social documents that talk about structural sin make very little use of Scripture. Yet the Bible gives many helpful examples of it. The prophet Amos provides a good place to start.

Amos's main concern, expressed as oracles directly from God, is the lack of economic justice among the people in Israel. He was a prophet in the eighth century BCE, a time of growth for the Israelites. We have evidence of increased economic activity and trade. We know of new types of houses being built that required complex social organization and excess money. From the perspective of archaeology, Amos's world looks like it would have been a time of human flourishing. Amos, however, points out that this prosperity was not shared among all the people. Wealth was built upon the backs of the poor, whom the rich exploited. We see this most clearly in Amos 8:

> Hear this, you that trample on the needy,
>   and bring to ruin the poor of the land,
> saying, "When will the new moon be over
>   so that we may sell grain;
> And the sabbath,
>   so that we may offer wheat for sale?
> We will make the ephah small and the shekel great,
>   and practice deceit with false balances,
> buying the poor for silver
>   and the needy for a pair of sandals,
>   and selling the sweepings of the wheat." (Amos 8:4-6)

Amos here offers a panoply of images and ideas that, with a little explanation, will be easy to understand. The first two lines are Amos's own words. Thereafter, Amos quotes the leaders in Israel, who say that they want their festivals and Sabbaths to come to an end. Why would they want the Sabbath to be over? The answer is nefarious: religious observance of the Sabbath requires not working, which would get in the way of economic activity. Their economic greed has overwhelmed their religiosity and faith.

A small ephah and big shekel indicate rigged weights and measurements; they will have "false balances" so as to make more money. This may seem strange to us, who live in a world in which weights and measurements are guaranteed. Such was not the case in the ancient world. Every culture had its own system of weights and measurements, and cheating was a constant danger. The poor were left to the whims of those who were in charge.

The problem in Amos's world is structural. He profiles an economic system that is skewed for the rich and powerful. Those without power suffocate, their freedom curtailed. It's not just an individual problem, but a broad social one that Amos critiques. A sinful world is one that pursues pure profit.

The words of Amos, rarely—if ever—invoked in church documents about structural or social sin, nevertheless sound quite similar to those of John Paul II. He says that "among the actions and attitudes opposed to the will of God, the good of neighbor and the 'structures' created by them, two are very typical: on the one hand, the *all-consuming desire for profit*, and on the other, *the thirst for power*, with the intention of imposing one's will upon others" (SRS 37). Amos would agree.

Benedict XVI also points to the economy as a primary place where the "pernicious effects of sin" are felt. He says that it is a myth that humans are self-sufficient and that our own actions alone cannot save us. In our search for material prosperity, we lose sight of true happiness and salvation. We assume wrongly that "the economy must be autonomous," an idea that has led humans "to abuse the economic process in a thoroughly destructive way" (CV 34). Ultimately, these systems and structures that humans have erected, Benedict says, "trample upon personal and social freedom, and are therefore unable to deliver the justice that they promise" (CV 34). Amos would agree.

Structural Sin in Paul's Letter to the Romans

We now jump to the New Testament for another exploration of structural sin. The beginning of Paul's letter to the Romans focuses a lot on sin. Figure 1 shows the frequency of the usage of the Greek word for sin throughout the New Testament. The huge spike corresponds to the first half of Paul's letter to the Romans. Paul, writing to a church he had not personally founded, nevertheless knows that there is tension in the community between Jew and Gentile. He explains that neither group has an advantage before God because sin is a problem for Jew and Gentile alike. The way sin is a problem, however, might surprise you. Consider the following examples:

> What then? Are we any better off? No, not at all; for we have already charged that all, both Jews and Greeks, are under the power of sin. (Rom 3:9)

> Where sin increased, grace abounded all the more, so that, just as sin exercised dominion in death, so grace might also exercise dominion through justification leading to eternal life through Jesus Christ our Lord. (Rom 5:20-21)

> But sin, seizing an opportunity in the commandment, produced in me all kinds of covetousness. Apart from the law sin lies dead.

I was once alive apart from the law, but when the commandment
came, sin revived and I died, and the very commandment that
promised life proved to be death to me. For sin, seizing an opportunity in the commandment, deceive me and through it killed
me. (Rom 7:8-11)

In each of these examples, sin *acts*. Paul makes sin the subject of the
sentences; it "does stuff." One scholar has referred to this part of Romans as sin's résumé.[8] This is sin personified, a verifiable actor—sin
with a capital "S." Paul does not talk about sin as an accumulation of individual choices. Sin, rather, is a cosmic force. The verbs Paul attaches
to sin indicate its menace. Sin increases, reigns, seizes opportunities,
deceives, and kills. Sin is not something to be taken lightly because
it lurks at the core of all that is wrong with the universe. This means
that humans get caught up in sin's snares regardless of our actions.
Simply being part of a sinful society can make us culpable, whether
we directly intend to commit a sin or not. Paul's analysis of what is
wrong with the world would be right at home in a Catholic encyclical
that discusses structural sin.

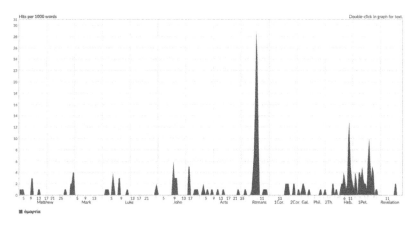

Figure 1. The frequency of the word "sin" in the New Testament. Note the spike in the first half of Romans. (Chart courtesy of Accordance Bible Software.)

8. Beverly Roberts Gaventa, "The Cosmic Power of Sin in Paul's Letter to the Romans," in *Our Mother Saint Paul* (Louisville, KY: Westminster/John Knox Press, 2007).

Overcoming Structural Sin

Scripture not only can help us identify and name structural sin, but it also provides us with guiding metaphors for its downfall. Amos envisions a violent response to structural sin. For Amos, the system is so rigged that the only solution is to dismantle the structures. Amos accomplishes this by alluding to the flood, which wiped humanity's slate clean and gave it a new beginning: "let justice roll down like waters, and righteousness like an ever-flowing stream" (Amos 5:24). These words, made famous in Martin Luther King Jr.'s booming baritone, call for a new beginning. Only a deluge of justice can meet the structural challenges of our day.

But Amos isn't done. In the eighth chapter he offers a series of images to describe what it is going to be like when God's justice shows up:

> I will make the sun go down at noon,
>   and darken the earth in broad daylight.
> I will turn your feasts into mourning,
>   and all your songs into lamentation
> I will bring sackcloth on all loins,
>   and baldness on every head;
> I will make it like the mourning for an only son,
>   and the end of it like a bitter day. (Amos 8:9-10)

Having already alluded to the flood, Amos now alludes to the plagues God brought upon Pharaoh in the book of Exodus. What should shock us here is that the plagues—here limited to darkness and death of the firstborn children—will be imposed on God's own people for their sins.

In the next chapter, Amos depicts God dismantling the Temple, dropping it stone by stone on the heads of the people:

> I saw the LORD standing beside the altar, and he said:
> Strike the capitals until the thresholds shake,
>   and shatter them on the heads of all the people;
> and those who are left I will kill with the sword;
>   not one of them shall flee away,
>   not one of them shall escape. (Amos 9:1)

Amos's solution to a structural problem is to pull down the structures and wash everything away.

Amos's reputation as a fiery prophet of God's judgment is well deserved. But the book does end with a ray of sunshine. Although scholars are pretty sure that the last few verses of the book are a later addition, they do give a glimpse of hope at the end:

> I will restore the fortunes of my people Israel,
>   and they shall rebuild the ruined cities and inhabit them;
> they shall plant vineyards and drink their wine,
>   and they shall make gardens and eat their fruit.
> I will plant them upon their land,
>   and they shall never again be plucked up
>   out of the land that I have given them,
>   says the Lord your God. (Amos 9:14-15)

Even Amos, perhaps the most pessimistic biblical author, does not end with annihilation. There is also here a path to a new life, an opening for transformation. Sinful structures must be condemned and abolished, but at the same time we must build up new spaces in which humans can flourish. After reading Amos, everyone will want a glass (or two) of the wine described here at its end.

Returning to the New Testament, in Romans 8, Paul culminates his discussion of sin's menace by talking about how God wins in the end:

> There is therefore now no condemnation for those who are in Christ Jesus. For the law of the Spirit of life in Christ Jesus has set you free from the law of sin and death. (Rom 8:1-2)

God, through Jesus, has "set us free." Jesus' life and death was a rescue mission, a liberation. We might initially think of this liberation in personal terms, and Paul certainly has that in mind. But Paul also gazes way beyond the personal horizon. The entire universe groans, hoping that "creation itself will be set free from its bondage" and "will obtain the freedom" that only God can provide (Rom 8:21).

As the letter continues, Paul contrasts a life in the flesh with a life in the spirit. We can live in the spirit because God has made it possible, by liberating us from sin. Time and again, Paul connects the spirit with "life."

> To set the mind on the flesh is death, but to set the mind on the Spirit is life and peace. (Rom 8:6)

> The Spirit is life. (Rom 8:10)

> For all who are led by the Spirit of God are children of God. . . . You have received a spirit of adoption. (Rom 8:14-15)

Our liberation, according to Paul, sets the conditions for life: a full life, a free life. Paul here does not just mean the "afterlife." He also has in mind the concrete conditions in which people live and how we act within the community. The images of life, peace, and adoption are precisely those conditions required for what Catholic social teaching would call the conditions for human development, for full flourishing.

While Amos and Paul are writing vastly different types of literature and are separated by a gulf of nearly eight hundred years, there is a parallel in their ideas. Both see the structural problem of sin and injustice—how it can be bred into the fabric of society. They both see the need for liberation from those structures. And, finally, both see that once liberation occurs, the conditions are set for authentic human flourishing.

Flourishing and the Prison-Industrial Complex

Unfortunately, we do not lack examples in our world in which human flourishing is diminished. I've chosen here to focus on our modern prison system. There are many ways our prison industrial complex might be seen as a structural sin. For example, it has problems related to racism[9] and it is excessively monetized.[10] Perhaps the best way to summarize and unite these problems is to suggest that prisons prevent human flourishing. They do not create conditions in which humans can "be great." And thus, incarceration will prove an instruc-

9. Donna Coker, "Foreword: Addressing the Real World of Racial Injustice in the Criminal Justice System," *Journal of Criminal Law and Criminology* 93, no. 4 (Summer 2003): 827–79.

10. See Angela Y. Davis, *Are Prisons Obsolete?* (New York: Seven Stories Press, 2003), especially chapter 5 on the prison-industrial complex.

tive test case for applying our understanding of sin to an example in our world today.

You may have seen the movie *The Shawshank Redemption*. It's a beautiful story about redemption, friendship, and life. It also reveals a dark truth about incarceration, its role in society, and how it ruins people's lives. Toward the end of the story, when long-time inmates are finally granted parole and some semblance of freedom, they realize that prison has occluded their future. The character played by Morgan Freeman states the truth about what prison does to people. Speaking about the walls of prison, he says, "First you hate 'em, then you get used to 'em. Enough time passes, you get so you depend on them. That's institutionalized." Though technically no longer behind bars, once freed they are still emotionally and mentally imprisoned. There is little that is "correctional" in a correctional facility. On the contrary, those who are or have been incarcerated find their ability to flourish destroyed.

Prison and the New Testament

Christianity started in prison. That might be a slight overstatement, but we often forget the role ancient law and punishment systems played in the origins of the faith. John the Baptist was imprisoned by Herod and beheaded. Jesus was arrested, tried, and executed by a process of Roman law (crucifixion was capital punishment for enemies of the state). Paul was also arrested and held, as were his coworkers Andronicus and Junia (see Rom 16:7). He wrote at least two letters while in prison. Signs in Philippi are happy to point tourists to the location of his prison, even though there is no archaeological evidence to support the spot as such (see fig. 2). John wrote the Book of Revelation while in exile on the island of Patmos, perhaps sent there as a criminal. He warns the church in Smyrna of their impending imprisonment (Rev 2:10).

The most dramatic stories in the New Testament about imprisonment are in the Acts of the Apostles:

- Near the book's beginning, all of the apostles are put in prison because of the high priest's jealousy. An angel of the Lord delivered them so they could continue their preaching (Acts 5:17-26).

Figure 2. Photograph near the spot traditionally venerated as Paul's prison in Philippi. Sixth-century Christian basilica in the distance. (Author's photo.)

- In Acts 12, Peter was arrested by Herod, put in chains, and surrounded by two guards. During the night an angel appeared, the chains fell from his wrists, and the angel led him away.

- In Acts 16, local magistrates stripped and beat Paul and Silas and put them in the innermost cell with their feet in the stocks. An earthquake freed them. On their way out they helped convert the jailer who had bound and beaten them.

- The closing sequence of Acts (chaps. 25–28) depicts Paul imprisoned and under guard, making his way to Rome, where he will appeal to the emperor. The book ends with him still under guard, preaching boldly, but with no resolution to his imprisonment.

We might say that the New Testament is prison literature.

Given the extent to which early Christians experienced imprisonment, it is no accident that in the Gospel of Matthew, Jesus included the incarcerated among those whom Christians must encounter: "I was hungry and you gave me food, I was thirsty and you gave me something to drink, I was a stranger and you welcomed me, I was naked and you gave me clothing, I was sick and you took care of me, I was in prison and you visited me" (Matt 25:35-36). This same idea is recapitulated in the book of Hebrews, where the author praises his audience: "for you had compassion for those who were in prison" (Heb 10:34). Later, the author gives a direct order: "remember those who are in prison, as though you were in prison with them" (Heb 13:3).

The "guilt" of our Christian ancestors reveals that God's law often runs afoul of human laws and institutions. Belief in God as creator and sustainer of life (as compared to the Romans who claimed the same role) put early Christians in opposition to the world order. In addition, acts of God that free prisoners, topple walls, break chains, and convert jailers suggest that the very idea of imprisonment is bankrupt.

These New Testament texts testify to two truths. First, blind trust in the justice of our justice systems may be naive. In the ancient world and at present, the system is rife with systemic problems. Second, the idea of incarceration is inimical to the Gospel. Imprisonment is built on grudge and retaliation, while Christian virtue is built on forgiveness and mercy. A Gospel of love and mercy was (and still is) at odds with a world built on grudge and retaliation.

Prison Today and Human Flourishing

For most of human history, incarceration was never thought of as punishment per se. It was a place where the accused were held until the sentence was meted out (often corporal punishment or some type of fine). Over the last two hundred years, incarceration itself has come to be understood as punishment.[11] Incarceration is now punitive, leading to loneliness, anxiety, stigma, and institutional violence. A person about to be released after two years in prison once shared with me:

11. See Davis, *Are Prisons Obsolete?*, 12–16.

"coming back here or death: they're both the same to me." Prison is not a place for flourishing.

You might ask: why should we care about the flourishing of a criminal? The answer: our pursuit of the common good must always be linked with the ability of life to flourish. Human dignity is never taken away, even if someone commits a heinous crime. The United States Conference of Catholic Bishops, in a statement on abolishing the death penalty, could equally have been critiquing our entire prison system when they said: "the pursuit of the common good is linked directly to the defense of human life. . . . Public policies that treat some lives as unworthy of protection, or that are perceived as vengeful, fracture the moral conviction that human life is sacred."[12]

Rather than a necessary institution to protect society, we tend to view incarceration as an "abstract site into which undesirables are deposited, relieving us of the responsibility of thinking about the real issues afflicting" the communities from which these people came.[13] Our society rarely asks why someone might commit a crime in the first place, if they were rightfully convicted, or what sorts of conditions persist that perpetuate crime. It is incumbent upon people of faith to try to improve conditions for all humans so that people can flourish. Individuals should be held accountable for their actions, but the church's social teaching would also compel us to think about the necessary "improvement of structures" for humans to live their best lives.[14]

There is little, if anything, about our current practice of incarceration that allows life to flourish. It does the opposite. I recently received training to become a mentor for people who are transitioning from incarceration back into society. As part of the training, we heard testimonies from various individuals who had been incarcerated. They talked about problems with housing, with finding a job, or with trying to avoid the "wrong crowd" so they don't fall back into bad habits. They struggled with addiction and loneliness. They are racked with debt and

12. United States Conference of Catholic Bishops, *A Culture of Life and the Penalty of Death* (Washington, DC, 2005), 14–15.

13. Davis, *Are Prisons Obsolete?*, 6.

14. Congregation for the Doctrine of the Faith, *Instruction on Christian Freedom and Liberation* (Libertatis Conscientia), March 22, 1986, https://www.vatican.va/roman _curia/congregations/cfaith/documents/rc_con_cfaith_doc_19860322_freedom -liberation_en.html.

financial obligations. I was most struck, however, when they talked about how people in society viewed them. They felt tainted; people viewed them with suspicion. Incarceration does not stop, I learned, when they leave prison. They bear the brunt of a society marked by sin and continue to feel its effects. To paraphrase Morgan Freeman in *The Shawshank Redemption*, they become "sinstitutionalized." A society where we don't pass on to others the forgiveness and mercy we ourselves have received does not embody the Gospel or the love of God.

The benefit of talking about social sin in the context of our criminal law system is that it names the deep attitudes necessary for seeking change. I find the words of Anna Rowlands to be instructive:

> To talk about social sin is not just to harp on in a dreary fashion about moral conduct but opens to us a series of practical actions and categories not typically present in political analysis: forgiveness, mercy, repentance and conversion.[15]

Concepts of forgiveness and conversion are precisely the elements that are lacking in our criminal law system. Yet they are the very attitudes and dispositions that should animate every Christian.

Scripture and Catholic social teaching tell us that individuals in and released from prison can't be ignored. To avoid sin, we need actively to seek them out, bringing near the tenderness of God's love and mercy. We can't say "well, I've never been in prison" and honestly claim to be without sin. Matthew 25 ("I was in prison and you visited me") and the rest of the New Testament will not let us off the hook. Nor will Pope Francis, who recently said "God's style is never distant, detached or indifferent. On the contrary, it is a style of proximity, compassion and tenderness."[16]

None of the attitudes entwined with prisons—retribution, monetization, or punishment—are Christian values.[17] Moreover, they lead

---

15. Anna Rowlands, *Towards a Politics of Communion: Catholic Social Teaching in Dark Times* (London: T&T Clark, 2021), 258.

16. "Pope: God's Style Is a Style of Proximity to the Most Vulnerable," *Vatican News*, April 2023, https://www.vaticannews.va/en/pope/news/2023-04/pope-gods-style-is-a-style-of-proximity-to-the-most-vulnerable.html.

17. See the thorough and theological treatment of Amy Levad, *Redeeming A Prison Society: A Liturgical and Sacramental Response to Mass Incarceration* (Minneapolis: Fortress Press, 2014).

to a system that destroys human lives. I would go so far as to suggest that our commitment to a Christian world should question whether prisons should exist at all. A world without prisons would require an entirely new society. It would require a society without racism. It would require a society that valued the image of God in every human. It would require a society in which it was almost impossible for people to fall into poverty. It would require a society in which drug treatment and mental health resources were available freely and quickly to anyone who is struggling. It would require a society in which all schools were equal in funding, resources, and facilities. I'm sure you can now see the point. A world without prisons would be an entirely new world. "Ultimately, it would require that in those unfortunate times when someone, filled with fury or despair, committed a crime, that we would face them not as objects—'criminals'—but as people."[18] A world without prisons would require a world in which personal and social sin was the exception, not the rule.

Conclusion

In the beginning, God told us to "be great" (Gen 1:28). In the end, God reveals a world to which all are invited: "Let anyone who wishes take the water of life as a gift" (Rev 22:17). In between is a world of sin that humans have built for themselves, in which too many do not have space for authentic flourishing. Any attempt to build a more just world, to accomplish the vision set forth by Scripture and the church's social teaching, first must recognize the problem of sin. Its antidotes are mercy, forgiveness, and love. We all need a conversion of heart, so that we meet every human animated by these virtues. We also need the courage to tear down sinful structures in order to build a world illuminated by the same. Humans are fragile, yet resilient. We will flourish if the conditions are right. As then Cardinal Ratzinger (who became Pope Benedict XVI) wrote when he was prefect of the Congregation for the Doctrine of the Faith, "the work of salvation is thus

---

18. Arthur Waskow, *Instead of Prisons: A Handbook for Abolitionists.* As quoted in Davis, *Are Prisons Obsolete?*, 45.

seen to be indissolubly linked to the task of improving and raising the conditions of human life in this world."[19]

Jesus, in the famous story of the woman caught in adultery, says to her: "from now on do not sin again" (John 8:11). When Jesus says "sin no more," we must take that to apply both our own personal sin, but also to the structures of sin that persist in our world. If we do not confront the places where sin dwells—both our own lives and in the structures of our society—we are not authentically living a Christian life and will have no hope of building a more just world in which every human has the ability to "be great."

---

19. *Instruction on Christian Freedom and Liberation* 80.

chapter 2

"The Weak Are Indispensable"

Solidarity in Action

If we have no peace, it is because we have
forgotten that we belong to each other.

—Mother Theresa

A fter every Mass we are dismissed with these words: "Go in peace, glorifying the Lord by your life." In a similar vein, at my parish we have a sign that you can only see as you leave the parking lot that says "Live it!" What do these phrases mean? How are we supposed to glorify God every day? What does it mean to live out our faith? The church does not leave us empty handed when trying to answer these questions. The church's teaching on solidarity, built on the foundation of Scripture, offers us a path for how to live our lives. Solidarity, however, is not well understood, and rarely consulted as Catholics navigate the modern world.

You may have seen a video of Derek Redmond, sprinter for Great Britain at the 1992 Olympic Games in Barcelona. He shredded his hamstring in the middle of the 400-meter race and went to the ground. The race finished around him, but he wasn't done. He got up and started limping around the track, pain and anguish on his face. As he continued on, a man emerged from the stands. It was Derek's father, who supported him and helped him along. The two crossed the finish line together.

I suspect most Catholics today have heard the word *solidarity*. I'm not sure how many know what it means. Even Pope Francis recognizes that the word *solidarity* today has become a "little worn and at times poorly understood" (EG 188). For some, solidarity calls to mind the protest song "Solidarity Forever," which supported unions in the struggle for labor rights in the interwar period. We have heard the word *solidarity* often during the protests against structural racism in 2020. Every time I watch a European soccer match, the players kneel before it begins. According to the commentators, the players want to be in solidarity with those who struggle against racism.

Songs can stir our emotions. Kneeling athletes can call attention to suffering. But solidarity is not just an emotion or a symbolic act. It "refers to something more than a few sporadic acts of generosity" (EG 188). Solidarity becomes real when someone, like Derek Redmond's father, sets aside the rules and expectations of our world and accompanies another on their journey, particularly one who is less fortunate or suffering. Solidarity must include "convictions" and "habits" that are "put into practice" (EG 189). Solidarity is not just a principle, but a virtue.[1]

Roman Catholics are supposed to build a world of solidarity and live accordingly. This chapter hopes to explain both what this means and why it is important. Solidarity begins with a "bond of interdependence between individuals and peoples" (CSDC 192). This bond exists because we are all made in the image of God. Solidarity becomes a reality, however, when people orient their lives around this reality. Jesus lived a life of solidarity, offering himself as a model for how to live one's life for others. Solidarity means more than a vague sense of unease at the suffering of others. It requires, as Jesus demonstrated, a concrete commitment to the authentic human development of all of God's creatures. Solidarity offers a path for how to "live it."

---

1. See Christopher P. Vogt, "Fostering a Catholic Commitment to the Common Good: An Approach Rooted in Virtue Ethics," *Theological Studies* 68 (2007): 399. For another good treatment, see Meghan J. Clark, *The Vision of Catholic Social Thought: The Virtue of Solidarity and the Praxis of Human Rights* (Minneapolis: Fortress Press, 2014).

"Do Nothing from Selfish Ambition": Solidarity in Scripture

While the Bible never uses the word *solidarity*, the idea is thoroughly biblical. Scripture testifies to the dignity of all peoples, who are made in the image of God. Solidarity begins at the beginning:

> So God created humankind in his image,
> in the image of God he created them;
> male and female he created them. (Gen 1:27)

Most ancient cultures thought the gods created humans as slaves. In Genesis we find something different: humans created to reflect God's image, to be God's presence in the world. All humans share equally in this image—it connects us all—which is why we need to be in solidarity with all other humans, both near and far.

In the New Testament, Jesus exemplifies solidarity. His insistence that we must lose ourselves for the sake of others, to serve rather than to be served, sounds a bass note for his entire ministry: "whoever wishes to become great among you must be your servant, and whoever wishes to be first among you must be slave of all" (Mark 10:43-44).

Jesus gives solidarity a practical bearing when talking about the need to love our enemies and give without expecting anything in return. It is easy, Jesus says, to love those who already love you back. The challenge lies in loving those who are hard to love: "love your enemies, do good, and lend, expecting nothing in return . . . for [God] is kind to the ungrateful [see Matt 5:45] and the wicked. Be merciful, just as your Father is merciful" (Luke 6:35-36). This quotation testifies to the need to treat all humans equally, both enemy and friend. No one is more or less deserving of God's mercy than anyone else. God showers mercy even upon the wicked and the ungrateful.

We see practical examples of solidarity in Jesus' parables. Perhaps the most famous of these is the parable of the good Samaritan. Luke introduces the parable with a conversation between Jesus and a lawyer. They agree that the two most important commandments are to love God with all your being and to love your neighbor as yourself (10:27). The lawyer then asks: "Who is my neighbor?" Jesus responds with the parable about a Samaritan who helps a man who had been beaten, robbed, and left for dead in the ditch. The Samaritan shows true solidarity by attending to the man and accompanying him. He pays for his care and even puts down money for any future expenses. The Samaritan takes from his own time and treasure to help someone whom he could have ignored. The lawyer's question, "who is my neighbor?" gets a shocking answer: *everyone*. It is not so much about the "who" but the "what"—solidarity is mercy in action.[2]

Jesus, of course, did more than talk and tell stories. He lived solidarity: "This is my body, which is given for you" (Luke 22:19). Jesus chose to offer all of himself. These words signify Jesus' radical solidarity with all humans. He did nothing for himself; he sought the good of others. In Philippians, Paul refers to Jesus' self-emptying. Jesus did not take advantage of his divinity, but:

> emptied himself,
>   taking the form of a slave,
>   being born in human likeness.
> And being found in human form,
>   he humbled himself
>   and became obedient to the point of death—
>   even death on a cross. (Phil 2:6-8)

Paul offers Jesus as a model for how Christians are supposed to live their lives: "Do nothing from selfish ambition or conceit, but in humility regard others as better than yourselves. Let each of you look not to your own interests, but to the interests of others. Let the same mind be in you that was in Christ Jesus" (Phil 2:3-5).

Jesus didn't just take a knee, offer thoughts and prayers, or change his Facebook picture as a sign of solidarity. He chose to accompany humanity. Emmanuel ("God with us") shows us a God in solidarity with humanity and gives us a life to emulate.

Solidarity is hard. We live in a world of division and strife. Our economy is built on selfishness, not altruism. We are told to accumulate, not give away. Solidarity does not play by the rules of the human game, and truly living it out will be difficult, if not dangerous. Paul was

---

2. Amy-Jill Levine, *Short Stories by Jesus: The Enigmatic Parables of a Controversial Rabbi* (New York: HarperOne, 2014), 113.

repeatedly beaten and imprisoned. In the Garden, Jesus prayed for a different path. His solidarity so challenged the powers of the world that he was sentenced to capital punishment—Roman crucifixion.

While Scripture is a clear resource and foundation for the church's understanding of solidarity, it also can be an impediment. Many biblical stories disregard the imprint of God's image in every human. The Bible condones slavery, portrays genocide, and devalues women. The church, too, has failed at solidarity. Christian crusaders and imperialists rampaged and colonized in a way that does not respect this teaching. The sex abuse crisis tells us that a church of fallible humans will never be a perfect witness to solidarity. Despite its failings, the church calls itself to renewal and continues to make a commitment to building a church and a world based on the reality that each human is "fearfully and wonderfully made" (Ps 139:14).

"A Firm and Persevering Determination": Solidarity in the Church's Teaching

The earliest documents in Catholic social teaching do not use the word *solidarity*, yet the idea is there. For example, in *Rerum Novarum*, Leo XIII tends to use the word *friendship*. He talks about how humans should "be united in the bonds of friendship, but also those of brotherly love" (RN 21).[3] He quotes 2 Corinthians 8:9, which says that though Jesus was rich, he became poor for our sakes. From this divine example, we can understand the "true dignity" of all humans (RN 20).

On the fortieth anniversary of *Rerum Novarum*, Pius XI built upon Leo's ideas. He utilizes the Pauline metaphor of the "body of Christ." While this phrase refers to the mystical body of the church, it also applies to the whole of society. Only when working from a sense of unity "will it be possible to unite all in harmonious striving for the common good, when all sections of society have the intimate convictions that they are members of a single family . . . that they are one body in Christ and 'severally members one of another,' so that 'if one

---

3. Pope Leo XIII, *Rerum Novarum*, May 15, 1891, in *Catholic Social Thought: Encyclicals and Documents from Pope Leo XIII to Pope Francis*, 3rd ed., ed. David J. O'Brien and Thomas A. Shannon (Maryknoll, NY: Orbis Books, 2016).

member suffers anything, all the members suffer with it'" (QA 137).[4]
Pius here utilizes Paul's metaphor of the body to explain the need for
a connection among all humans. This call for unity defines the very
concept of solidarity.

The Second Vatican Council published *Gaudium et Spes* to address
the plight of humanity and offer remedies from the heart of the church.
It identifies individualism as one of the key problems facing our world:
"no one, ignoring the trend of events or drugged by laziness, [should]
content himself [or herself] with a merely individualistic morality."
On the contrary, "the obligations of justice and love are fulfilled" only
if each person contributes to the common good "according to his [or
her] own abilities and the needs of others" (GS 30).[5] This critique of
individualism contributes to a proper understanding of solidarity. If
our morality starts with concerns pertaining to ourselves, we have
missed the need to be working for the common good of all.

Gaudium et Spes also insists that God created humans for social
unity, not for isolation. God saves us "not merely as individuals, without any mutual bonds, but by making [us] into a single people" (GS
32). Salvation is corporate, and so we must dispel any myth that one
person can work out her or his own salvation without thinking about
the good of the whole.

Pope Paul VI gives a full-throated charge to the church when he
discusses solidarity in *Populorum Progressio*. He calls for "mutual
understanding and friendship" and says we must "begin to work together to build the common future of the human race" (PP 43). This
work is for individuals, communities, and nations. He turns to Jesus'
parable about the rich man and Lazarus (Luke 16:19-31), calling for a
world where Lazarus, who is poor and sore-ridden, can sit at table with
the rich man. He describes what it would take and the kinds of actions
that would be required to achieve such a new level of social unity:

> This demands great generosity, much sacrifice, and unceasing
> effort on the part of the rich man. Let each one examine his [or

---

4. Pope Pius XI, *Quadragesimo Anno*, May 15, 1931, in *Catholic Social Thought*,
ed. O'Brien and Shannon.

5. Pope Paul VI, *Gaudium et Spes*, December 7, 1965, in *Catholic Social Thought*,
ed. O'Brien and Shannon.

her] conscience, a conscience that conveys a new message for our times. Is he prepared to support out of his own pocket works and undertakings organized in favor of the most destitute? Is he ready to pay higher taxes so that the public authorities can intensify their efforts in favor of development? Is he ready to pay a higher price for imported goods so that the producer may be more justly rewarded? Or to leave this country, if necessary and if he is young, in order to assist in this development of the young nations? (PP 47)

Paul VI here interrogates all Catholics and people of goodwill who would claim that their faith is their own, individual prerogative. Solidarity teaches that we are all connected and we need to be ready to change our lives for the good of the other.

Finally, we turn to John Paul II, who continues to sharpen and develop the church's teaching on solidarity. In his encyclical *Solicitudo Rei Socialis*, he offers a thorough evaluation of solidarity. Solidarity "is not a feeling of vague compassion or shallow distress at the misfortunes of so many people, both near and far. On the contrary, it is *a firm and persevering determination* to commit oneself to the *common good*; that is to say to the good of all and of each individual, because we are *all* really responsible for *all*" (SRS 38). Here we recognize the challenge of solidarity. It is about more than just pangs in the heart. It requires concrete action, moving out from oneself, and offering oneself fully:

> In the light of faith, solidarity seeks to go beyond itself, to take on the *specifically Christian* dimension of total gratuity, forgiveness and reconciliation. One's neighbor is then not only a human being with his or her own rights and a fundamental equality with everyone else, but becomes the *living image* of God the Father. . . . One's neighbor must therefore be loved, even if an enemy, with the same love with which the Lord loves him or her; and for that person's sake one must be ready for sacrifice. (SRS 40)

The love of God that saved us requires our own love for others in return. Our own salvation requires concrete actions on behalf of other people. To claim to be "saved" and not be concerned about the dignity of other humans portrays a misunderstanding of how and why Jesus came in the first place. As *Gaudium et Spes* dramatically states: "The

Christian who neglects his [or her] temporal duties neglects his duties toward his neighbor and even God, and jeopardizes his [or her] eternal salvation" (GS 43).

Scripture and church teaching offer us a robust understanding of the concept of solidarity as a Christian virtue. Built on the foundation of Jesus' own teaching and life, Christians are called to live with the same self-giving posture. Solidarity requires a thorough, life-altering commitment to the good of others, even those far away or those whom we might consider our enemies. Solidarity, Paul VI says, "imposes a duty" (PP 17).

Ultimately, our understanding of solidarity comes from God. Christian theology understands God as the Trinity: three persons in one God. Benedict XVI highlights the importance of our understanding of the Trinity for our understanding of solidarity because it models the simultaneous truths of unity and individuality:

> The Trinity is absolute unity insofar as the three divine persons are pure relationality. The reciprocal transparency among the divine Persons is total and the bond between each of them complete, since they constitute a unique and absolute unity. God desires to incorporate us into this reality of communion as well. . . . Relationships between human beings throughout history cannot but be enriched by reference to this divine model. (CV 54)

In other words, God's very self models solidarity: a relational living for the other, bonded together into a complete unity. The way we model the image of God is not just a static concept, but is something into which we must live. Divine dignity must be seen as "something we *possess* and something we *become*."[6]

Paul, Solidarity, and the Body of Christ

On a warm, sticky night in the thick of the COVID-19 pandemic, my neighborhood took advantage of some road work that closed our street. At dusk, several neighbors carried armloads of wood into the road and started a bonfire. Most people on the block joined the fes-

---

6. Anna Rowlands, *Towards a Politics of Communion: Catholic Social Teaching in Dark Times* (London: T&T Clark, 2021), 55.

tivities. Beer and wine flowed. The fire was enormous. Chairs were gathered. Conversations started.

This revelry also coincided with the 2020 election. When the topic came up, some people groaned and said "NO POLITICS." I pushed back because I thought decent, thoughtful adults should be able to have civil conversation. I was wrong.

I ended up in a lengthy conversation with a man who lives down the street. He grew up Roman Catholic and attended Catholic schools (as did his kids). As we conversed, it became clear to me that he and I agreed on very few things. Several of the topics of political conversation cut to the heart of Catholic teaching. For example, we had a long conversation about immigration. He insisted that he bears no responsibility for the well-being of people in other countries. He did not appreciate me pointing out that his opinion did not conform to the church's teaching on solidarity.

How could this be my neighbor? How could we inhabit the same street, city, state, and country? How could we both count ourselves as members of the same church? If I had a hard time feeling connected and united with him, how much harder it must be to feel a bond of unity with people in other parts of the planet.

I presume you feel this, too. There are deep divisions among us. We see them among our neighbors, coworkers, friends, and even family. How many people have you blocked or unfriended on Facebook or other media platforms because of their views? Have you felt frustrated because the homily did not hit the political point you wanted to hear? (That would never happen to me!) Have you felt outraged because someone did (or didn't) wear a mask during the pandemic? Is there any place nastier than #CatholicTwitter? We "follow" and "like" the wrong things. We assume the worst of each other. We never forgive. We can't find common ground. We don't listen. We are not unified. We seek our own good, work to vindicate our own point of view, put ourselves first rather than the other. Sometimes, the hardest person to love is the one with whom you share a fence.

If you are exhausted at the divisions in our world, the apostle Paul feels your pain. While he does not have a magic elixir that will immediately make us all successful in solidarity, he does understand the problem and offer solutions. In what follows, we will look at Paul's metaphor of the body as a way to deepen our understanding of solidarity.

Many Parts, One Body

Ancient people thought a lot about body parts. In Corinth, people flocked to the temple of Asclepius when their parts failed. The infirm or injured would offer a sacrifice to the god and then sleep overnight in the temple. As the person slept, Asclepius would appear to her or him in a dream and provide a cure for the ailment. After being healed, the individual would offer a clay model of that body part in thanksgiving to the god. The museum in Corinth has a room reserved just for these clay body parts (see fig. 3 and 4). The small room is packed with clay models of ears, hands, feet, legs, torsos, genitalia, breasts, arms, and heads. There are many parts.

When Paul says in 1 Corinthians 12 that there are many parts but one body, the people in the church may have immediately thought about the clay body parts at the Asclepius temple. Paul reassembles those parts, asking his community to consider how they can all fit together. There is just one body.

Paul first makes a biological observation: no body part can claim independence. Each part has a role to play, and each role is integral to the functioning of the whole. God gave each part a specific purpose. Even if a part of the body were so arrogant as to assert its independence, "that would not make it any less a part of the body" (1 Cor 12:16).

Paul then claims that diverse body parts comprise the body's strength and abilities. These parts depend upon each other: "If the whole body were an eye, where would the hearing be? If the whole body were hearing, where would the sense of smell be?" (1 Cor 12:17). God made and arranged the body in an intentional way, each member with its role and place. The eye cannot say to the hand, "I have no need of you" (1 Cor 12:21). Each part depends on the others.

Paul's final way of using the body metaphor is counterintuitive. When I go for a walk in the winter my fingers turn numb first because they are not essential. I can live without fingers but I can't live without a heart or a brain. Paul turns this biological reality on its head. He claims that we should pump blood to the extremities: "the members of the body that seem to be weaker are indispensable, and those members of the body that we think less honorable we clothe with greater honor, and our less respectable members are treated with greater respect" (12:22-23). Those parts that seem unimportant—the appendix or a

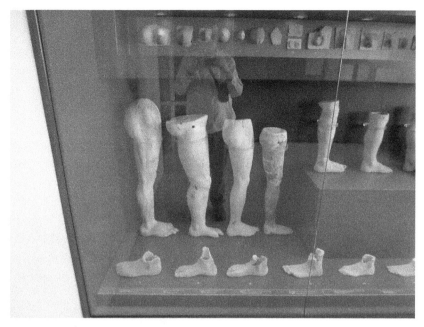

Figure 3. Clay body parts from the temple to Asclepius in Corinth. (Author's photo.)

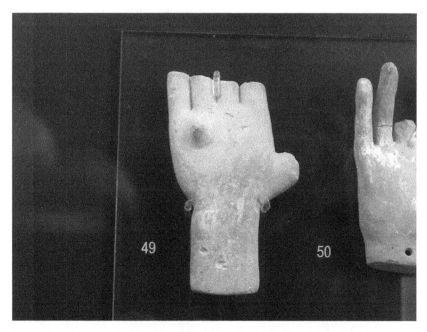

Figure 4. Clay hands dedicated to Asclepius in Corinth. (Author's photo.)

toenail—are those we should give the highest due. The dispensable extremities become paramount.

Ultimately, Paul wants unity: that "there may be no dissension with the body" and that the members "may have the same care for one another" (1 Cor 12:25). He achieves this unity through solidarity: all parts should consider the whole first. We should all share together in the joys and sufferings of the body: "If one member suffers, all suffer together with it; if one member is honored, all rejoice together with it" (1 Cor 12:26). As he says in Galatians: "Bear one another's burdens, and in this way you will fulfill the law of Christ" (Gal 6:2). Communal pain, trauma, suffering, joy, and celebration are marks of the body of Christ.

Solidarity, in Paul's body metaphor, does more than call for unity. Unity is achieved by the strong working on behalf of the weak. Unity is a prerequisite, of course, but the real burden is placed on the strong to uplift the weaker members. We must protect and empower the weaker members.

Back to the Bonfire

How might Paul's insights be applied to the bonfire conversation with my neighbor? There is no doubt, of course, that Paul and the church's teaching on solidarity would ask my neighbor to reconsider his position on immigration. If we are all connected and called to live a life of solidarity, then we bear responsibility for the well-being and flourishing of all. My neighbor might be considered a strong member of the body because he lives a comfortable life in a rich country. He ought to care about the weaker member.

On the other hand, we should not miss the irony of the theology professor accusing someone of insufficiently understanding or living the church's teaching. In 1 Corinthians 8, Paul warns against just such a problem. Here Paul discusses those in the community who are struggling to understand and live out the church's teaching. (The issue in this case is food that has been sacrificed to an idol, but that's beside the point.) Paul says that the strong, those who understand, must always make provision for those who don't get it. Paul's warning for the strong is harsh: "By your knowledge those weak believers for whom Christ died are destroyed. But when you thus sin against members of your family, and wound their conscience when it is weak, you sin against Christ" (1 Cor 8:11-12).

Paul's metaphor of the body, and the church's teaching on solidarity, would ask me to count my neighbor as among "the weak." I can hear the voice in the back of my mind: "But he doesn't deserve it!" "He's a jerk." "He doesn't care about others the way he should." Precisely. If I make a haughty critique of his views because I think I understand the teaching better, I perpetuate the very division Paul is trying to quash.

Looking deeply at Paul's metaphor of the body does not immediately fix things. It can't compel people to be in solidarity with the poor or the immigrant. It doesn't force me to extend love and friendship to my neighbor. It does, however, show the deep roots of the concept within Christian theology. It also opens the door to one place where we might find common ground amidst our divisions: contemplating the body of Christ in the Eucharist.

Eucharist and Solidarity

Every Roman Catholic who attends Mass and partakes of the Eucharist is confronted with the line "the body of Christ." How many of us contemplate the depth of Paul's use of the body metaphor at that moment? Do we connect solidarity with the Lord's Supper? Do we allow the words "given for you" to shape our actions towards others? John Paul II ends his encyclical about social concern by making just such a connection:

> All of us who take part in the Eucharist are called to discover, through this sacrament, the profound *meaning* of our actions in the world in favor of development and peace; and to receive from it the strength to commit ourselves ever more generously, following the example of Christ, who in this sacrament lays down his life for his friends. (SRS 48)

To partake of the Eucharist is more than a moment of individual piety, but a declaration of solidarity with God's whole body. Partaking of the body of Christ imposes a duty and responsibility that we live as if we are part of that body. Paul provides the practicalities of that way of living: it is about more than just unity. In the body of Christ, those who are marginalized and overlooked become the center of concern. The weak are indispensable.

Spin Rates and Solidarity

There are many issues we could explore in an effort to make solidarity relevant in our world today. Modern problems related to war, the environment, racism, or poverty all require action spurred by solidarity. I want to focus on one particular aspect of our world that may not immediately come to mind: sports. Youth sports, in particular, are an opportunity to build a world of solidarity, but the reverse is increasingly the case: youth sports are exacerbating problems of poverty and division in the world today.

One beautiful spring day I sat on the Iowa prairie, but I couldn't see the horizon. I was in a gymnasium, back aching, knees cramped, watching my son play travel basketball. We were a three-hour drive from home. We had spent $120 on a hotel room. There were further outlays for gas, food, and entrances. As I wandered the 300,000 square foot, $45 million Des Moines RecPlex that weekend, I couldn't help but wonder: Who are all these people? Where did they come from? Why do they spend money on this? Who might be excluded?

Sport is an essential part of human culture. It allows us to express ourselves; to practice rigor and endurance; and to build community. Too often, however, our sport contributes to and exacerbates the problems in our society. For many families today, youth travel teams are a parental obligation. We participate without thinking about it and feed a behemoth industry worth an estimated $19 billion per year.[7] What should be a beautiful expression of creation and an opportunity for community becomes exclusive and costly.

Youth sports ought to be the perfect training ground for solidarity. At the start of every Little League season I tell the players and parents that "baseball is about relationships." Nobody has any idea what I mean, and those who know me roll their eyes. But it's true. A team comes together to work toward a common goal. All have to participate and think about the good of the whole. Teammates demonstrate empathy toward one another. The best player might need to set aside her or his own individual progress to help others improve. Sadly, our

---

7. "Commercialization of Youth Sports," University of Kansas Online Sport Management Program, https://onlinesportmanagement.ku.edu/community/commercialization -of-youth-sports.

sports are increasingly bereft of solidarity. We view them more for personal gain than community building. Dobie Moser calls this the "sports as ladder to success" model of participation.[8] As handpicked travel teams become the norm, the poor are left out. If sport presents us with an opportunity for solidarity, we swing and miss.

Case in point: in the 2022 World Series, there were no American-born black players.[9] While there are a variety of factors that created this situation, one culprit is the privatization of travel baseball. As more and more families leave affordable community-based organizations like Little League, there are fewer opportunities for poor or marginalized communities to participate. To quote one recent commentator on this situation: "Baseball is becoming a mostly white country-club sport for upper-class families to consume, like a snorkeling vacation or a round of golf."[10] Baseball is now "America's pastime" only in an ironic sense: it mirrors the inequality we see in society.

I have seen this firsthand. Every spring when we start to rake the fields and draft the teams for our local Little League chapter, some of last year's players are gone. No one has to ask where they went. We all know they've chosen travel teams instead. Some of these travel teams feed into high schools, but others are private teams organized by parents. It can cost a player's family as much as $2,500 to participate for one season.[11] I know families who travel every weekend of the summer for baseball. A friend of mine sold their family cabin because "we can never get there because of the baseball schedule." I have seen footage from high-speed cameras on large-screen iPads analyzing the minutiae of a twelve-year-old's swing. A travel baseball patriarch once asked me: "Do you know the spin rate on your son's fastball?"

What, you may be wondering, does sports and travel baseball have to do with our Catholic faith? In 2018, the Vatican Dicastery for the

---

8. Dobie Moser, "Catholic Youth Organization Sports: A Mission-Oriented Focus," in *Youth Sport and Spirituality* (Notre Dame: University of Notre Dame Press, 2015), 200.

9. Barry Sverluga, "Why Black Players Are Disappearing from the World Series," *The Washington Post*, November 1, 2022, https://www.washingtonpost.com/sports/2022/11/01/black-players-world-series/.

10. John W. Miller, "How America Sold Out Little League Baseball," *America Magazine*, May 19, 2022.

11. Miller, "How America Sold Out Little League Baseball."

Laity, Family and Life published a lengthy document attempting to answer just this very question. They titled it "Giving the Best of Yourself: A Christian Perspective on Sport and the Human Person." The idea of "giving" provides a foundation for how we should think about sports. Too often, however, our youth sports today have become about "taking." This document will help us connect how we think about youth sports and solidarity.

Leaving our Cocoons

Pope Francis once spoke about how nobody likes it when one player "devours the ball," someone my kids would call a "ball hog." All sports require teamwork and insight into different roles and positions. The team doesn't work if everyone is selfish. Francis continues: "To belong to a sports club means to reject every form of selfishness and isolation, it is an opportunity to encounter and be with others, to help one another, to . . . grow in brotherhood."[12]

Any time we are able to demonstrate the kind of fraternity that Francis describes here—a genuine encounter with others—God will be involved. As theologian Richard Gaillardetz writes:

> Sports can create an enormous capacity for empathy with one's teammates, and that empathy, in turn, generates a deep sense of team solidarity. Why is this empathy of spiritual significance? Because it is the human capacity to care for others, to move out of the cocoon of our own self-absorbed existence, that is the basis for human love. . . . There is no human movement toward the other in an act of love, caring, or compassion in which God is not implicated.[13]

Think about what happens when an injury occurs during a game. The game stops. Everyone takes a knee. In that moment we are in solidarity, even with members of the opposing team. We have left our cocoons and adjusted our actions on behalf of another; they have become part

---

12. Dicastery for Laity, Family and Life, "Giving the Best of Yourself," 3.3, https://press.vatican.va/content/salastampa/en/bollettino/pubblico/2018/06/01/180601b.html.

13. Richard Gaillardetz, "For Love of the Game: Toward a Theology of Sports," in *Youth Sport and Spirituality*, 174.

of our circle of concern. During a 2022 football game between the Buffalo Bills and Cincinnati Bengals, Damar Hamlin's heart stopped, and so did the game. It was never played. Two teams, which seconds earlier had been trying to dominate the other, were now on the same side—the human side.

Being part of a team can help us to get outside of ourselves and encounter others. But it doesn't stop there. Catholic teaching would push us to translate our understanding of teamwork and encounter beyond our "team." We need to radiate this same solidarity to the wider world: "Solidarity, in the Christian sense . . . goes beyond the members of one's own team."[14] Sports can become a training ground for the wider world. The focus on team and the good of the whole should teach us lessons we can take into the real world.

Sacrifice

Although the sacrifice bunt is disappearing from baseball, we laud "sacrifice" in sports all the time. Players "put their bodies on the line" or "take one for the team." These phrases refer to personal sacrifice oriented toward winning or the benefit of the team. Rarely, however, does that sacrifice extend to a world of solidarity in which we sacrifice for the good of those who are less privileged. Why do we value sacrifice on the field and then forget it when outside the lines? It is our duty to "clothe with greater honor" those members who are "less honorable" (1 Cor 12:23).

Pope Francis expresses this same sentiment, that our sports must never forget those at the margins of society. In an address to a global conference on faith and sports in 2016, he said: "I am also thinking about those many children and the youth who live at the edges of society. Everybody is aware of the enthusiasm with which children will play with a rugged old deflated ball in the suburbs of some great cities or the streets of small towns. I wish to encourage all of you . . . to work together to ensure these children can take up sport in circumstances of dignity, especially those who are excluded due to poverty."[15] Given

14. "Giving the Best of Yourself," 3.9.
15. Pope Francis, "Sport at the Service of Humanity," Pontifical Council for Culture, http://www.cultura.va/content/cultura/en/eventi/major/sport/francis0.html.

the church's teaching on solidarity, Francis's words here ought to apply to all people of faith who want to enact in the world the love they have first received from God. When we participate in sports, our Catholic faith and its teaching on solidarity should compel us to ask: Who is included and who is excluded by how, when, and where we play?

Rights and Responsibilities

Most individuals and families, of course, are not malicious when making decisions about sports for their children. People think of themselves as free to make choices that are best for themselves. Freedom, however, must always be yoked with responsibility: "Many people believe that freedom is doing what one wants, without any limits. Such a view decouples freedom and responsibility and may even eliminate regard for the consequences of human acts. However, sport reminds us that to be truly free is also to be responsible."[16]

Those who assert their own rights, John XXIII says, and ignore their duties, are like people who "build with one hand and destroy with the other" (PT 30).[17] The body of Christ, in Paul's formulation, leaves no place for rights divorced from duties. In Colossians he says that the whole body is "held together by its ligaments and sinews," strong, stringy connections that bind us together (Col 2:19). Our mutual connections place burdens of concern. Being a part of the body means we have responsibilities; we can't claim independence or ignorance. In Galatians, Paul tells us that we are called for freedom, but that we should not use freedom as an "opportunity for self-indulgence" (Gal 5:13). Youth sports have increasingly become about taking rather than serving. We view them as some sort of weird ladder to success rather than an opportunity to build the world of solidarity that God demands of us.

Live It!

Living with true solidarity will seem crazy and unorthodox. The pressure today is to be a good consumer and conform. Of course my son

16. "Giving the Best of Yourself," 3.2.

17. Pope John XXIII, *Pacem in Terris*, April 11, 1963, in *Catholic Social Thought*, ed. O'Brien and Shannon.

should play travel baseball. Why shouldn't he? His friends will be there. Shouldn't he have the best?[18] Such thinking evinces a logic of privilege and lacks solidarity with those who are impacted by our actions.

In his letter to the Romans, Paul says, "do not be conformed to this world, but be transformed" (Rom 12:2). This type of transformation would mean living as if we are all one body, where we honor and prioritize the less honorable parts. Forces of economic pressure and self-aggrandizement push in the opposite direction. Living with true solidarity would mean leaving behind exclusionary practices, but also working on behalf of those who have been excluded. A life of solidarity would work to ensure that all children can take up sports with dignity, especially those excluded by poverty: "the general rights of a life in dignity and freedom must be protected in sports. They apply in particular to the poor and the weak."[19]

Solidarity is about more than equality. It requires concrete self-giving on the behalf of others—opponents, neighbors, or enemies. This self-giving could be applied to any number of sinful structures in our world; sport is only one example, and it may seem a trivial one. But the need to live with solidarity cuts to the core of our salvation in our requirement to share just as God shared with us. As Benedict XVI says, "true solidarity—though it begins with an acknowledgement of the *equal* worth of the other—comes to fulfillment only when I willingly place my life at the service of the other . . . just as Jesus 'humbled himself' so as to give men and women a share in his divine life."[20]

I return to the questions with which we began this chapter. What does it mean to glorify the Lord with our lives? How can we "live it"? Sports can help us think about how to be an outgoing church and how to live a life of solidarity: "More than many other platforms, sport brings together the downtrodden, the marginalized, the immigrant, the native, the rich, the powerful and the poor around a shared interest and at times in a common space."[21] We should take notice if we find ourselves in situations where groups are excluded or unable to

18. See Moser, "Catholic Youth," 200.

19. "Giving the Best of Yourself," 4.1.

20. Benedict XVI, "Address to the Participants of the Pontifical Academy of Social Sciences," May 2008, https://www.vatican.va/content/benedict-xvi/en/speeches/2008/may/documents/hf_ben-xvi_spe_20080503_social-sciences.html.

21. "Giving the Best of Yourself," 5.1.

play. Sports practices built on equality and inclusion might be a good place to start glorifying the Lord with our lives, to show that when we partake of the body of Christ and say "amen," we mean it.

chapter 3

"You Are Not Your Own"

The Universal Destination of Goods

The earth is the LORD's and all that is in it.
> —Psalm 24:1

Thank God for the things I do not own.
> —Theresa of Avila

I magine a room of bleary-eyed eighteen-year-olds less than excited for their 9:00 AM theology class. I walk in, knowing we are about to have a challenging discussion about the church's teaching on private property. I start by picking on someone. I ask: "Do you own that Apple watch?" The answer is always, "Yes." I follow up with some questions: How do you know you own it? (I bought it.) Where did you get the money? (My job.) How are you able to work a job? (My brain/strength/ work ethic.) Where did those things come from? (I practiced/my parents taught me.) My questions continue until the student catches on and says, "I guess it all came from God originally."

"It all came from God" nicely summarizes the church's teachings on property and possessions. Everything is a gift from God, and nothing truly belongs to us. If the goods of the earth were bestowed upon us by God, then they belong to everyone equally. This teaching, often called the "universal destination of goods," will seem crazy in our world today. Of course we own our stuff! We bought it, we paid for it, we wear it, and we operate it.

In this chapter, we will explore the church's teaching about possessions and how Scripture can contribute to and enrich that teaching. The church repeatedly affirms that the right to private property is not an absolute right. We should not own property beyond what is needed for survival and a life of simplicity. Ownership must always be measured against the common good. In various ways, Scripture also attests to the truth that our possessions are not truly our own.

"The Land Is Mine . . .": Scripture and Possessions

Many texts in the Hebrew Bible call for the sharing of the goods of the earth. In some cases, laws promulgate a system where excessive accumulation of possessions would be impossible and against God's wishes.

Leviticus 25 offers precepts and laws related to the land and ownership. Every seven years the land should lie fallow, modeled on God's rest on the seventh day of creation. Such a law places limits on accumulation by suggesting the land has a higher purpose, something beyond monetization.

Every fifty years Leviticus calls for a more radical reset, called a *Jubilee.* At the fifty-year Jubilee, all land returns to its original owner. Because of this, any purchase of land is only temporary. All purchases were calculated according to the number of years left until the next Jubilee. In essence, people were not buying land so much as leasing its harvests and goods until the next Jubilee, when the system would reset. Such laws and practices undermine accumulation of wealth and property. The justification for these laws is simple: "The land shall not be sold in perpetuity, for the land is mine; with me you are but aliens and tenants" (Lev 25:23). The land is God's; humans can never truly own it. The Sabbath and Jubilee laws provide a precedent for limits on personal ownership of property based on God as the true owner and provider of all.

The New Testament takes up similar ideas and applies them to individuals. At the beginning of the Gospel of Luke, John the Baptist offers fiery rhetoric: "every tree therefore that does not bear good fruit is cut down and thrown into the fire" (Luke 3:9). The crowds, rightly terrified by such a statement, want to know: "what then should we do?" John's response is all about possessions: "Whoever has two coats must share with anyone who has none; and whoever has food must do likewise. . . . Be satisfied with your wages" (Luke 3:11, 14).

Later in Luke, Jesus tells a parable about a rich man perplexed at how to store all his possessions. He pulled down his barns and built bigger barns. God responds to this individual: "You fool! This very night your life is being demanded of you. And the things you have prepared, whose will they be?" (Luke 12:20). The summary Jesus provides of this parable needs little interpretation: "Be on your guard against all kinds of greed; for one's life does not consist in the abundance of possessions" (Luke 12:15).

These biblical examples offer ample justification for thinking about ownership and possessions. Whether applied to society as a whole, or to individuals, a life in communion with God requires us to think about what we own and how much. These texts suggest that our relationship with God—and even our eternal destiny—intertwines with our accumulation of possessions.

"No One Is Rich by Nature . . .": Possessions and the Early Church

In the earliest centuries of the church, leaders and theologians took scriptural ideas and the teachings of Jesus and applied them to people's lives. They did not back away from the radical claims about ownership, property, and possessions offered in Scripture. Clement of Alexandria (d. 220 CE), for example, argues that the goods of this world are common to all and alludes to the parable from Luke 12 that we discussed above:

> God brought our race into communion by first imparting what was his own . . . and made all things for all. All things therefore are common, and not for the rich to appropriate an undue share. That expression, therefore, "I possess and possess in abundance: why then should I not enjoy?" is suitable neither to human beings, nor to society. (*Paed.* II.13)[1]

---

1. Clement of Alexandria, *The Instructor*, book 2, *Early Christian Writings*, https://www.earlychristianwritings.com/text/clement-instructor-book2.html.

Clement's logic here is not hard to follow. God gave us God's very self, both in creation and in the incarnation of Jesus. From these gifts flow our existence and all good things. Who are we to say, in light of this gift, that we own any part of it?

Early church figures also looked to nature for clues about God's intentions. They fixated on the fact that all are born naked, with no possessions. Moreover, the dead can't take possessions to the afterlife. These realities should teach us something about the intentions of the Creator. Ambrose of Milan, for example, notes that "no one is rich by nature, for nature begets everyone as poor. Indeed we are neither born with garments nor are we begotten with gold and silver." He goes on to say that we cannot enclose all our possessions in a tomb: "[nature] knows not how to enclose within the tomb the expansive boundaries of one's estates [or] the excessive extremes of one's possessions" (*Nab.* 14).[2] To put this in modern terms: nobody is born wearing an Apple watch, and no one can drive their BMW to heaven.

Such thinking led to some even more direct statements. Basil (d. 378 CE), for example, asserts: "To the hungry belongs the bread that you keep. To the naked belongs the clothing that you store in your closet."[3] John Chrysostom (d. 407 CE) says something similar: "Wealth is not a possession, it is not property; it is a loan for use."[4]

We have, then, in the earliest centuries of the church, a clear and consistent set of teachings that all things are a gift from God. Excessive accumulation and ownership contradict this teaching. Anyone who accumulates beyond what meets their immediate needs is not just being greedy but impeding creation as God intended it.

Catholic Social Teaching and the Destination of Goods

The social convulsions and plight of the poor created by the industrial revolution prompted the first great Roman Catholic social document, *Rerum Novarum* (1891). An important component of Pope Leo XIII's treatise is its teaching on possessions and the destination of goods.

---

2. As quoted in Daniel G. Groody, *Globalization, Spirituality, and Justice: Navigating a Path to Peace*, rev. ed. (Maryknoll, NY: Orbis, 2015), 69.

3. *Patrologica Graeca* 31:277–78; as quoted in Groody, *Globalization*, 71.

4. *Patrologica Graeca* 62:556; as quoted in Groody, *Globalization*, 73.

Leo notes that possessions are permissible, but then emphasizes that any excess possessions need to be used charitably. He quotes Thomas Aquinas, who said that a human "should not consider his [or her] outward possessions as his own, but as common to all, so as to share them without difficulty when others are in need" (RN 19). Leo sees the church as a place where rich and poor are drawn together and where they have a duty to each other, especially the duty of justice (RN 19).

Leo's teaching about the universal destination of goods has been reaffirmed and built upon by every pope since. On the fortieth anniversary of *Rerum Novarum*, Pius XI noted that a person's "superfluous income is not left entirely to his [or her] own discretion. . . . On the contrary, the grave obligations of charity, beneficence and liberality which rest upon the wealthy are constantly insisted upon in telling words by Holy Scripture and the Fathers of the Church" (QA 50). Pius's phrase "grave obligations" ought to grab our attention. These teachings are not presented as an option for people to consider. The universal destination of goods is not presented as "food for thought." This teaching comes to the rich and the comfortable as a "grave obligation," as something on which salvation hinges. To paraphrase John the Baptist, the axe is ready to chop down any tree that does not bear good fruit.

On the hundredth anniversary of *Rerum Novarum*, John Paul II wrote *Centesimus Annus*, continuing the church's tradition of social teachings. While noting that Leo and the church affirm the right to private property, the church also teaches that private property "is not an absolute right" because of how the church understands the use of goods. While humans have freedom to use goods as they see fit, that freedom is always "subordinated to their original common destination as created goods" (CA 30).[5] This shows continuity with Leo's formulation, that the goods we receive from God do not fully belong to us, but are intended for the benefit of all, for the common good.

Few people will appreciate the idea that we should have limits on our possessions. One common retort to the teaching of the universal destination of goods is: "I worked hard for it, so it's mine." My students often say: "Other people can have what I have if they work for it." While

---

5. Pope John Paul II, *Centesimus Annus*, May 1, 1991, in *Catholic Social Thought: Encyclicals and Documents from Pope Leo XIII to Pope Francis*, 3rd ed., ed. David J. O'Brien and Thomas A. Shannon (Maryknoll, NY: Orbis Books, 2016).

these sentiments are understandable, John Paul II has an answer for such a claim: the world is not set on a level playing field.

> The fact is that many people, perhaps the majority today, do not have the means which would enable them to take their place in an effective and humanly dignified way within a productive system in which work is truly central. They have no possibility of acquiring the basic knowledge which would enable them to express their creativity and develop their potential. They have no way of entering the network of knowledge and intercommunication which would enable them to see their qualities appreciated and utilized. Thus, if not actually exploited, they are to a great extent marginalized. (CA 33)

It is a sad truth that some people do not have the opportunity to improve their station in life because of the situations in which they live. Over the last few years, I have come to be friends with a refugee from Myanmar. My friend's son, still in Myanmar, was about to start at a technical high school, but a military coup shut down the schools. His son now has nothing to do. There is little work, no education, and no free press. His future has been destroyed; he has no opportunity for self-realization. This is the type of situation that leads John Paul II to say that today, many people do not have the means to actualize their full human dignity. The world is not level.

The church has never taught that there is a connection between hard work and the right to accumulate possessions. On the contrary, the burden lies upon those with possessions, even if acquired through extremely hard work, to ensure that the marginalized have a chance at a satisfied life, so that all can flourish as God intends. Because of the suffering of so many, "it is a strict duty of justice and truth not to allow fundamental human needs to remain unsatisfied, and not to allow those burdened by such needs to perish" (CA 34).

We have only scratched the surface; there are dozens of other places where church teaching reaffirms and further develops the idea of the universal destination of goods. The phrase itself, "the universal destination of goods," is rather clunky. It might be easier to think of it as the "law of simplicity and charity." All Christians are called to live a simple life without excess. Any accumulation of goods or wealth beyond what supplies a simple life are required to be passed on to those in need; it is a "grave obligation." As formulated by Paul VI in *Populorum Progressio:* "private property does not constitute for anyone an absolute and unconditioned right. No one is justified in keeping for his [or her] exclusive use what he [or she] does not need, when others lack necessities" (PP 23). In other words, the common good is always a "check" on private ownership. The common good always has priority.

Paul and Possessions

We turn now to a deeper dive into Scripture to look at some places where the universal destination of goods can be supported and developed. In this case, our ally will be perhaps a surprising one: the apostle Paul. At two points in his ministry, Paul offers striking support for the "universal destination of goods." While these texts are never fully utilized in the church's teaching, a deep look at what Paul says and why will support the idea that we should not accumulate possessions and push the church's teaching in some new directions.

No Hoarding of the Manna

When Paul of Tarsus suddenly joined the church—which he had been persecuting—you can imagine the skepticism. He probably would have received the eyeroll emoji. After a few years of successful ministry, he was summoned by the church leaders in Jerusalem to an inquisition. Church leaders wanted to make sure he was really on their side and that he properly understood and practiced the Gospel. Paul passed this test and church leaders approved of his ministry to the Gentiles. When the proceedings were wrapping up, they added one more requirement: that he should "remember the poor." Paul says that he was "eager to do" this very thing (Gal 2:10). Woven into the fabric of Paul's ministry, therefore, was a constant call for generosity and the need to share God's gifts. Paul refers to this collection in his letter to the Galatians, in both letters to the Corinthians, and in the letter to Rome. In other letters he alludes to the generosity of the churches in Thessaloniki and Philippi. The first great Christian mission, therefore, included ministry to and support for the poor.

I suspect most Roman Catholics have never heard about Paul's collection for the poor. It never plays a starring role in any of the church's social documents, so far as I can tell. *Rerum Novarum* does note that Paul "hesitated not to undertake laborious journeys in order to carry the alms of the faithful to the poorer Christians," which are called "deposits of piety" (RN 24). The lack of attention to Paul's collection is unfortunate, because both its method and theological justification perfectly support the church's teaching about the universal destination of goods.

In 2 Corinthians 8-9, Paul discusses his collection for the poor. He begins by laying a guilt trip on the Corinthians. He notes how generous the neighboring churches in Macedonia have been. The grace of God, he says, has been granted to the churches of Macedonia because "their extreme poverty" has "overflowed in a wealth of generosity" (2 Cor 8:2). He lauds the Macedonians for how they "voluntarily gave according to their means, and even beyond their means" (2 Cor 8:3).

After this cajoling, Paul encourages the Corinthians to emulate not only the Macedonians, but Christ himself, who "though he was rich, yet for your sakes he became poor, so that by his poverty you might become rich" (2 Cor 8:9). Christ becomes a model of self-giving that created the Corinthians' new spiritual reality. This spiritual reality should be reflected in the physical world as well. The Corinthians should enflesh the spiritual gifts they have received by giving their material goods to the poor.

Paul justifies the Corinthians' need to share their wealth by turning to the story about manna in the book of Exodus. When the Israelites were wandering in the desert after the escape from Egypt, God provided food for them. Each morning, when "the layer of dew lifted, there on the surface of the wilderness was a fine flaky substance" (Exod 16:14). Moses explains that this substance is bread that God has given them. Moses instructs them to gather it up, only as much as each person needs—no hoarding allowed. Those who disobeyed and tried to keep some for the next day found that their saved portions bred worms and became foul. God arranged the entire situation so that no matter how much each one gathered, they all had precisely what they needed and nothing more. The people were not allowed to collect anything beyond what they needed each and every day.

Possessions, for Paul, are like manna in the desert. This explains how he can tell the Corinthians that "it is a question of a fair balance between your present abundance and their need, so that their abundance may be for your need, in order that there may be a fair balance" (2 Cor 8:13-14). This balance needs to exist because of what the story in Exodus teaches: "the one who had much did not have too much, and the one who had little did not have too little" (2 Cor 8:15). The gifts of God are for everyone, and no one may accumulate beyond what their immediate needs would dictate.

You Are Not Your Own

Paul also talks about ownership and possessions in 1 Corinthians, but here it involves our very selves:

> Do you not know that your body is a temple of the Holy Spirit within you, which you have from God, and that you are not your own? For you were bought with a price; therefore glorify God in your body. (1 Cor 6:19-20)

He repeats the same phrase in the next chapter: "you were bought with a price" (1 Cor 7:23).

Paul here applies words of commerce to human beings, employing language from the ancient slave trade. While today we might recoil at such language—even if metaphorical—we need to consider slaves and their place in the ancient church and wider world in order to understand Paul's message. Slaves were part of the early church. Paul's letter to Philemon, for example, discusses a slave named Onesimus who was an integral part of the community and very close to Paul (we will visit this situation in some depth in chapter 5). Slaves may have been attracted to the message of freedom in Paul's preaching and joined the church on their own. On the other hand, if they were owned by a rich family that hosted a church in their home, slaves might have been in the church's midst by compulsion.

Ancient Greece and Rome, the civilizations that moderns look back upon with wonder and awe, were built by slaves. During Paul's lifetime, it is likely that 10 to 20 percent of the Roman population were slaves, which would amount to tens of millions of souls. Rome's entire history likely saw over one hundred million people enslaved. People could become slaves through war, by birth, or by selling themselves to get out of debt.

The boundaries around slavery in the ancient world were permeable. A slave could be released from his or her owner and become a "freedperson" (see fig. 5). Corinth, in particular, was known for having a large number of freedpersons, and we know they were among civic leaders there. Corinth's association with slavery and freedpersons was so strong that one ancient author called the city a "mass of good-for-nothing slaves."[6]

Figure 5. Retaining wall at ancient Delphi inscribed with the names of freed slaves. (Author's photo.)

Imagine a church in Corinth meeting in the home of a wealthy family who owns slaves. When Paul says "you are not your own" and "you were bought with a price," humans become objects. This language, in a world with ubiquitous slavery, would sadly have been familiar to

6. See Laura Salah Nasrallah, "'You Were Bought with a Price': Freedpersons and Things in 1 Corinthians," in *Corinth in Contrast: Studies in Inequality* (Leiden: Brill, 2013), 60.

everyone. Paul applies the language to everyone in the church, slave and slave owner alike. All are placed metaphorically upon the *statarion,* the stone block on which slaves were bought and sold.[7] When Paul says "you are not your own," he asks each member of the church to stop thinking of him or herself as master of their own destiny and to think of themselves as a commodity.

A marble relief carving, part of a funerary monument from around 50 BCE in the area of Thessaloniki, gives us a concrete image to contemplate in the context of Paul's language about ownership (see fig. 6). The carving depicts eight people, four full size and four who are diminutive. The small figures are not children; they are slaves. Not only are they smaller, but they are carved with lighter relief. They live in the background, in only two dimensions. Paul's language suggests that we think of ourselves not as those figures protruding from the marble, thrusting themselves into the center of affairs. Rather, we should take our place in the background, humbling and debasing ourselves because we are not our own.

Figure 6. A grave stele from near ancient Thessaloniki (c. 50 BCE) depicting a family with four slaves in the background. (Author's photo.)

Paul's language about ownership finds ultimate justification in the life of Jesus. If we are bought, the purchase comes through God's

7. Nasrallah, "You Were Bought with a Price," 72.

self-giving love for humanity exemplified in the death of God's son. In Galatians, Paul writes that Christ "loved me and gave himself for me" (Gal 2:20). This self-giving becomes the model for the apostles: "To the present hour we are hungry and thirsty, we are poorly clothed and beaten and homeless, and we grow weary from the work of our own hands. . . . We have become like the rubbish of the world, the dregs of all things, to this very day" (1 Cor 4:11-13). Paul and the other apostles, in imitating Christ, have become the lowest of the low.

Jesus made himself low, which provides a model for the apostles and the church. Ultimately, Paul applies the metaphor of slavery and buying and selling of humans (as problematic as it may be) to explain the foundational motivator for all Christian ethics. Before any other decision or choice, we must first think of ourselves as not our own. God has bought us. Captured us. Claimed us. We have done nothing to deserve this. We may not have even wanted it; it happened while we were still sinners (see Rom 5:8). God owns us and we do not own ourselves. We belong to God and to one another.

We tread on thin ice in attempting to find something positive in Paul's language about slavery. Paul's letters were used by slave owners in the United States to justify that gross injustice. Paul himself was never enslaved, and so many modern theologians question whether he has a right to talk about slavery, or even use it as a metaphor.[8] Despite its past misuse, I would contend that because Paul's language about slavery can contribute to our understanding of possessions, it is worth reclaiming it in this limited way.

Paul offers theological ideas that enrich our understanding of the universal destination of goods. If we operate as if we own ourselves, believing that we author our own destinies, then problems with greed, comfort, and luxury will quickly follow. However, true self-giving, living as if we are slaves to Christ, will undermine any undue accumulation of possessions and free us up to live for others.

How to Live Your "Best Life"

I'm writing this at the public library. I happen to be sitting close to the self-help section. Here are some of the titles I see on the shelves:

---

8. See, for example, Angela Parker, "One Womanist's View of Racial Reconciliation in Galatians," *Journal of Feminist Studies* 34, no. 2 (2018): 23–40.

- *Your Story Is Your Power*
- *Be Yourself*
- *The Greatest You*
- *Creating Your Best Life*
- *Superhuman*
- *The Happiness Equation*
- *Get a Life That Doesn't Suck*
- *How to Be Fine*

While I would appreciate a life that "doesn't suck," these titles point to the general emphasis of the world and culture today. We're all trying to figure ourselves out, to live our best lives. We put ourselves at the center. Our world is constantly looking for a life hack, the secret, that will unlock happiness and fulfillment.

Scripture and Catholic social teaching would ask us to think differently. The Gospel and a life of faith have never been about personal fulfillment. Did Jesus live his best life? Did Mary solve the happiness equation? Was Paul a superhuman? Were they fine and fulfilled? Did they elevate themselves and seek happiness? A world of self-care, of bath bombs and man caves, runs the risk of missing the essential duty of living the Gospel in the real world—that we are not our own, and our possessions and our very selves need to be directed towards others. I do not mean to suggest we should disregard our bodies or our mental health. Overemphasis on the self, however, enables habits that allow us to forget the source and destination of all that we have, even our very selves.

Any suggestion today that we do not own ourselves, that we can't craft our own story and future, will seem crazy. It clashes with everything else we are told. As Paul says, the message of the cross is "foolishness" (1 Cor 1:18); it does not work according to the world's logic. Paul knows that many in the Corinthian church were not of high birth:

> Consider your own call, brothers and sisters: not many of you were wise by human standards, not many were powerful, not many were of noble birth. But God chose what is foolish in the world to shame the wise; God chose what is weak in the world to shame the strong; God chose what is low and despised in the world, things that are not, to reduce to nothing the things that

are, so that no one might boast in the presence of God. He is the
source of your life in Christ Jesus. (1 Cor 1:26-30)

Living as if we are not our own will clash with the logic of the world.

Realizing we are not our own, our disposition always must be
toward the one who is less fortunate. In very simple terms, we must
think of the good of the other, the common good of all, before we
think of our own good. Precisely because we are not our own, we
belong to God and to others. As Paul says later in 1 Corinthians: "the
members of the body that seem to be weaker are indispensable, and
those members of the body that we think less honorable we clothe
with greater honor, and our less respectable members are treated with
greater respect. . . . But God has so arranged the body, giving the
greater honor to the inferior member" (1 Cor 12:22-24).

Paul's thinking here reminds me of the words of the *Catechism*:

> Having become a member of the Church, the person baptized
> belongs no longer to himself, but to him who died and rose for us.
> From now on, he is called to be subject to others, to serve them
> in the communion of the Church. (CCC 1269)

If Paul's teaching is true with regard to our own lives, how much more
must it apply to our possessions? Paul's words apply equally to spiritual realities and physical property: "What do you have that you did
not receive? And if you received it, why do you boast as if it were not
a gift?" (1 Cor 4:7).

Paul, it turns out, offers a robust affirmation and foundation for the
church's teaching on the universal destination of goods. We own nothing. It all comes from God, even our very selves. We are not our own.

Ownership and the Housing Crisis

It's hard to think of a teaching that would conflict with our society
more than the universal destination of goods. Our entire economy
is built upon the desire for accumulation. Pay attention to advertisements. They never focus on having "just enough" or "meeting your
needs." They're all grounded in the logic of luxury and personal ag-
grandizement: Quiet. Relaxation. Speed. Excess. Beauty. Strength.
Companies associate their products with these ideas because humans

run to them. Eugene McCarraher refers to the world of advertisements as being like icons. Ads "visibly disclose an invisible reality . . . which is exactly what the stained glass windows" in a church are trying to do. He continues: "Within advertising's symbolic universe, under capitalism, your spiritual formation has the particular end of accumulation, how to make the most money possible. Heaven is a fat bank account."[9]

Imagine showing up at someone's home and telling them that their second car belongs to the poor. Imagine asking someone to give away all but one pair of shoes. How would you convince someone that their house is too big and an immigrant family will be moving in? We also ought to think about our "me time" and "free time" as not belonging to ourselves. These are the very actions and questions that the universal destination of goods would ask of us.

Catholic social teaching offers principles and guidelines; it rarely gives specific policy proposals. The principles of the teaching remain timeless, particularly so if they do not get mired in politics and specifics. These documents also regularly note that people of good will can come to varying practical applications of these teachings. The teachings are clear, but how to live them out and make them effective may prove contentious. People open to dialogue and with good intentions can have honest disagreements about how best to implement an idea like the universal destination of goods. In what follows, I will focus on one particular issue where the teaching on the universal destination of goods would challenge the world in which we literally, physically, live: our houses.

Our Houses of Hewn Stone

The prophet Amos has something to say about houses, but I don't think he could have survived as a realtor. Amos is known as the social justice prophet par excellence. God's word comes to him with fire and anger at the way the rich and powerful are exploiting the poor. (Recall his stance on structural sin that we explored in chapter one.) God announces woe upon those who are at ease and lounging in luxury (see Amos 6:1-7). There will be consequences for the rich and powerful, who are trampling the poor and taking their food (5:10-11). Amos

9. Eugene McCarraher, "Enchanted Capitalism," *Plough Quarterly* 36 (2023): 40.

announces to these people: "you have built houses of hewn stone, but you shall not live in them" (5:11). This one phrase, "hewn stone," says it all. A house of cut rock in Amos's time is a sign of luxury. To build such structures required quarries, transportation infrastructure, skilled labor, precise tools, and excess capital. Go ahead and build them, the prophet says, but you will not live in them. This is a critique and a warning to a society that takes pride in possessions and does not make provisions for the poor.

Were Amos alive today, he would not have to change his tune. We have many problems with housing. Worldwide, housing prices are rising too fast for most families.[10] Homelessness is a persistent problem, impacting both individuals and entire families.[11] Far too many people live in "precarious housing" situations.[12] There is a clear link between housing and other issues of health and justice.[13] In the United States we have tax and zoning policies that create inequality between rich and poor communities.[14] Affordable housing is out of reach for so many Americans that one scholar has coined the phrase "unaffordable America."[15]

There is a direct connection between the housing choices of many middle-class and affluent Americans and local and global housing crises. Many people in the United States view their homes as an investment whose value will appreciate over the years. This skews the market not only for poor families in the Unites States, but for the entire global system. For example, the economic crash in 2008 was fueled primarily by a runaway housing market. Shaky mortgages were

---

10. International Monetary Fund, "Housing Research," https://www.imf.org/external/research/housing/index.htm.

11. Marian Wright Edelman and Lisa Mihaly, "Homeless Families and the Housing Crisis in the United States," *Children and Youth Services Review* 11 (1989): 91–108.

12. Kelly Green and Johanna Brugman Alvarez, "Precarious Housing, Health and Well-Being across Diverse Global Settings," *Global Discourse* 12 (2022): 247–54.

13. Mark L. G. Jones, "Tenure Security, Housing Quality and Energy Injustice in Dhaka's Slums," *Global Discourse* 20 (2022): 1–32.

14. "Addressing Challenges to Affordable Housing in Land Use Law," *Harvard Law Review* 135, no. 4 (February 2022), https://harvardlawreview.org/print/vol-135/addressing-challenges-to-affordable-housing-in-land-use-law/.

15. Matthew Desmond, *Unaffordable America: Poverty, Housing, and Eviction* (London: Routledge, 2022).

being packaged into swaps and speculations.[16] When this seized up, the entire planet was thrown into a severe recession and crisis, which had an outsized impact on the poor.[17] This entire system is driven by a mythological desire for the "American Dream." Own a big house! Two cars! Three TVs! Safe neighborhood with good schools! At the same time, this crisis laid bare the global imbalances and showed a "lack of real concern for human beings" (EG 55).

Once a family is ensconced in a large, comfortable home, the problems continue. A good portion of American homes are crass examples of overconsumption. Since the 1970s, the average house size in the United States has increased by 43 percent, while the average number of inhabitants per house has decreased by 15 percent.[18] About 45 percent of the energy costs in a residential home support heating and cooling. We're building bigger and bigger houses with rising energy costs, yet fewer people are living in them.

Social Housing: A Proposal

Catholic social teaching ultimately calls for authentic human development. The goal of the church and its members should be the improved living conditions for all of God's creatures. Undue accumulation and impious spending habits preclude such development. As Pope Francis says in *Laudato Si'*: "Authentic human development has a moral character. It presumes full respect for the human person, but it must also be concerned for the world around us and 'take into account the nature of each being and of its mutual connection in an ordered system.' Accordingly, our human ability to transform reality must proceed in line with God's original gift of all that is" (LS 5). In other words, all our efforts to make a better world need to start with the recognition of all we have been given by God.

16. Stephan Dieckmann and Thomas Plank, "Default Risk of Advanced Economies: An Empirical Analysis of Credit Default Swaps during the Financial Crisis," *Review of Finance* 16, no. 4 (2012): 903–34.

17. Martin Feldstein, "The Global Impact of America's Housing Crisis," *Project Syndicate* (2009).

18. Center for Sustainable Systems, "U.S. Environmental Footprint Factsheet," University of Michigan, 2023, https://css.umich.edu/publications/factsheets /sustainability-indicators/us-environmental-footprint-factsheet.

What can we do? Do I expect every Roman Catholic with a sub-urban house that is even slightly bigger than necessary to sell their homes? I won't answer that question, although Jesus does (see Mark 10:17-27)! There are people and organizations who are thinking practically about how to change the situation. One proposal is called "Social Housing 2.0." Scholars and social scientists aim to rethink housing with three organizing principles: that it is non-speculative (i.e., not meant for accruing value); that it is democratically run; and that it is publicly backed. Their aims are ambitious:

> Social housing challenges a fundamental article of faith among much of the public, many policymakers, and elected officials: that the primary function of housing is as a private asset that can be bought, sold, and speculated on. By reframing the conversation to include its broader social value, governments and communities can prioritize housing goals beyond maximizing its economic value in the market. Housing sits at the nexus of numerous societal problems, and as a result, social housing is uniquely poised to address important issues beyond merely providing shelter. Social housing can address segregation, environmental and climate crisis, racial and economic exclusion, community cohesion, and others.[19]

Catholic social teaching would certainly support the idea that housing is a human right, not a commodity for enriching the rich. While large-scale social and structural changes for equitable housing seem daunting, they will never become a reality if most people do not adjust their thinking with regard to possessions. If we think we own ourselves and our possessions, the poor will always be left wanting and the homeless will never have homes.

Benedict XVI reminds us that *"every economic decision has a moral consequence"* (CV 37). Today we make moral judgments about housing, but the wrong ones. We judge the homeless, not those living in homes that are too big. We judge those with houses in the wrong part of town, not those who have benefited from a global system skewed to enable the rich in their excess. News stories regularly cover the cost

---

19. Gianpaolo Baiocchi and H. Jacob Carlson, "Social Housing 2.0: Viable Non-Market Tools for Today's Housing Crisis," *Pathfinders* (April 2022), 7.

of housing and its availability. Rising interest rates always get coverage. Rarely do the homeless make it to the headlines. When did you last read about the shantytowns in Dhaka? Into such a situation, Paul whispers: "you are not your own." He reminds us to thank God for the "indescribable gift" (2 Cor 9:15) we have all been given. Since everything has been given to us, Scripture and the church's social teaching place a grave obligation on us to consider God's gifts as common to all.

chapter 4

"Revolution of Tenderness"

The Preferential Option for the Poor

He raises the poor from the dust,
    and lifts the needy from the ash heap,
to make them sit with princes,
    with the princes of his people.

—Psalm 113:7-8

"Because the poor are despoiled, because the needy groan,
    I will now rise up," says the LORD;
    "I will place them in the safety for which they long."

—Psalm 12:5

The drive home after Sunday Mass. Hangry kids in the back seat. An exhausted musician and liturgist to my right. And in the driver's seat, the biblical theologian, frustrated because he didn't have control of the day's homily. I should be smart enough to let us ride home in silence. Instead, I vent.

One of the texts (among many) that I often see misinterpreted is the story of Jesus' temptation by the devil. While Mark narrates this story in only a couple of verses, Luke and Matthew give almost identical extended versions. Jesus refutes each of the devil's three temptations by quoting Scripture. It is worth quoting the passage in full:

> Then Jesus was led up by the Spirit into the wilderness to be tempted by the devil. He fasted forty days and forty nights, and afterwards he was famished. The tempter came and said to him, "If you are the Son of God, command these stones to become loaves of bread." But he answered, "It is written,
>> 'One does not live by bread alone, but by every word that comes from the mouth of God.'"
>
> Then the devil took him to the holy city and placed him on the pinnacle of the temple, saying to him, "If you are the Son of God, throw yourself down; for it is written,
>> 'He will command his angels concerning you,' and
>> 'On their hands they will bear you up,
>>> so that you will not dash your foot against a stone.'"
>
> Jesus said to him, "Again it is written, 'Do not put the Lord your God to the test.'"
>
> Again, the devil took him to a very high mountain and showed him all the kingdoms of the world and their splendor; and he said to him, "All these I will give you, if you will fall down and worship me." Jesus said to him, "Away with you, Satan! for it is written,
>> 'Worship the Lord your God, and serve only him.'" (Matt 4:1-10)

Most homilies on this text will understandably focus on temptation. The "take away" message usually claims that we will be tempted like Jesus. And, like Jesus, we can overcome that temptation with Scripture and prayer.

Turning such an interpretation over in my mind on the drive home from Mass, I'm unsatisfied. I find it arrogant to stick "us" right into Jesus' place in the story. Jesus is not like "us." As the Son of God—divine and human—the things that tempt him might look nothing like what tempts "us." I might be tempted to gossip, to slander, to get angry, or to lust. But I can never be tempted to use the power of God to gain temporal power. I can never be tempted to turn a stone into a morsel of bread. I can't be tempted to command a legion of God's angels to protect me. In this story, the differences between Jesus and "us" impress me more than the similarities.

If we import ourselves directly into the story, we run the risk of missing other insights into our world for which the text might be crying out. In particular, this story should tell us something essential about what it means to live a Christ-like life. In rejecting these temptations, Jesus did more than avoid making the wrong choice. He also actively chose a way of living. By not making bread, by avoiding personal power, and by choosing contingency rather than security, Jesus showed us the path of life. Jesus actively chose poverty, hunger, and vulnerability.

Ignoring my better instincts, I vocalize my frustrations in the car: "Why can't the homily ever mention the social aspects of the Gospel? Is it too much to expect the priest to understand the larger truths in the story of the temptation? Does it always have to be about 'us?'" Eye rolls from the back seat.

Despite the fact that I subject my family to these rants on a regular basis, my point stands. And I'm not alone. Fr. Joseph Wresinksi, who started a group called "Fourth World Movement" working with communities in extreme poverty, thinks our interpretations of this story are too "cautious." He suggests that we misinterpret because we do not want to think about how a Christian life should be incongruous with a life of comfort. He summarizes the situation this way:

> The only explanation I can find for our cautious interpretations and our reluctance to accept the magnitude of [Jesus'] sacrifice is our own fear of seeing Him choose absolute vulnerability and of having to follow Him even that far.[1]

In his responses to the temptations, Jesus actively chose a way of living: radical vulnerability. Here is where we can put "us" into the story. The choices Jesus made set a task for all of us, but we are afraid of following him on such a path.

Jesus choosing poverty and vulnerability in the temptation story exemplifies advocacy for the poor throughout Scripture. The Bible consistently insists that God carries a special care for the poor. God's love of the poor is a truth to which "the whole tradition of the Church bears witness" (SRS 42). This aspect of God's love has come to be known as the "preferential option for the poor."

The preferential option for the poor is about more than intellectual understanding. This option also must apply "to our social responsibilities and hence to our manner of living" (SRS 42). Because God chooses the

---

1. Joseph Wresinski, *Blessed Are You the Poor!*, trans. Alwine de Vos van Steenwijk and Diana Skelton-Faujour (Paris: Fourth World Publications, 1992), 26.

poor, so must we. What, in practical terms, does it mean to choose the poor, to live out the preferential option? Recently canonized as a saint, Óscar Romero gives language to what the option for the poor means:

> I am talking about an authentic option for the poor, of becoming incarnate in their world, of proclaiming the good news to them, of giving them hope, of encouraging them to engage in a liberating praxis, of defending their cause and of sharing their fate.[2]

What Romero describes here is precisely what Jesus did in rejecting the devil's temptations. Jesus chose to share the fate of the poor.

Because of this call to be with and share the fate of the poor, Peter Maurin once said that we should "blow the dynamite of the church." What he means is that the church's teaching about the poor is explosive. The concept of "becoming incarnate" in the world of the poor and of "sharing their fate" will challenge the very foundations of our lives. Put on your crash helmet; the fuse has been lit.

Signs of the Times

In the summer of 2001, I worked in New York City with the "Fourth World Movement," an organization dedicated to "overcoming poverty by seeking out people living in the worst economic conditions and exclusion."[3] Five days a week I took a sixty-minute train ride and two or three subways from pristine Princeton, New Jersey, to some of the poorest neighborhoods in the United States. We tried to build relationships with kids and families in order to foster community and to help them advocate for themselves, especially at the United Nations.

I was tasked with helping one family in particular: "Mrs. Z" and her six children. My first visit to their family in the Bronx was one I will never forget. Their tenement apartment was like a prison: buzzing to unlock doors and everything encased in iron bars. Once I reached their apartment, Mrs. Z was not present. The six kids (the oldest was about

2. Óscar Romero, "The Political Dimension of the Faith from the Perspective of the Option for the Poor," in *Liberation Theology: A Documentary History*, ed. Alfred T. Hennelly (Maryknoll, NY: Orbis Books, 1990), 298.

3. ATD Fourth World, "Overcome Poverty," https://www.atd-fourthworld.org/who -we-are/overcome-poverty/.

twelve) had free rein of the two-bedroom apartment. There was one big pile of clothes in the living room. The toilet was stopped up and smelled foul. There was no food. This image is seared into my memory: cries and whooping of the children, stench, and an overwhelming sense that these living conditions were inhumane.

I spent all day with the kids. We bought bananas and yogurt. We took the subway to a park where there was a free concert. We found a splash park. As daylight faded, I had to return to Princeton. I brought the children back to their apartment and eventually had to leave them as I had found them, still with no word from their mother.

I recount these experiences not to tout my exploits, but to relate how that summer impressed on me the importance of "seeing." One of the foundations of Catholic social teaching is the "signs of the times." This means that Christians need to have an awareness of the problems of injustice in our world; we need to know what is happening. The beginning of *Gaudium et Spes*, the Vatican II document about the church's place in the world, proclaims that "the Church has always had the duty of scrutinizing the signs of the times and of interpreting them in the light of the gospel. . . . We must therefore recognize and understand the world in which we live, its expectations, its longings, and its often dramatic characteristics" (GS 4). The signs of the times requires us to experience the world and also to utilize scientific disciplines, which give us data and statistics about social problems in our world.

When it comes to the issue of poverty, true "seeing" is harder than it might appear. Zoning laws and property tax regulations keep rich and poor separate from each other. For example, Mrs. Z's apartment in the Bronx projects was only a short subway ride away from Yankee Stadium—physical proximity, yet conceptually an ocean apart. Unwritten codes also regulate our behavior. Anyone who has visited Davenport, Iowa, has heard the phrase "Don't go south of Locust." Locust Street was the segregation line in town and now serves as a not-so-veiled warning to avoid the poor. We have constructed a world in which the rich are never confronted with the poor; it takes work to "see."

The Fourth World Movement recently published a research report with Oxford University called "The Hidden Dimensions of Poverty."[4]

---

4. ATD Fourth World and the University of Oxford, *The Hidden Dimensions of Poverty*, October 2019, https://www.atd-quartmonde.org/wp-content/uploads/2019/12/Hidden-Dimensions-of-Poverty-20-11-2019.pdf.

The global testimonies of people in persistent poverty included in this document help give voice to some of what I observed during my one summer in the Bronx:

> "Poverty feels like a tangled web that you can never escape." (p. 15)

> "You can't get to sleep, you're thinking 'what can I do?' What am I going to feed my children? You feel really bad; it hurts here inside." (p. 17)

These are anecdotal statements that can help us "see" what poverty is like.

Statistics and the social sciences also help us discern the "signs of the times." According to Oxfam, every four seconds, a human on our planet dies because of poverty and inequality. Ninety-eight percent of the world's population lives below the United States poverty line, which is about $33 per day. Seventy percent of people in our world live on less than $10 per day. (I just spent $4 on the coffee I'm drinking while I write this.) At the same time, the eighty richest people in the world have as much combined wealth as the poorest 3.5 billion people.[5]

Although the statistics above are important, we also need to recognize that poverty is about much more than just having enough money. Even the term *poverty* "hides more than it reveals."[6] Poverty has a "multidimensionality" that cuts across various aspects of our world. Experts who study worldwide poverty assert that focusing on income alone will not produce policy that actually addresses its core issues. Poverty involves a lack of access to clean water, healthy food, and basic services such as education and electricity. A better way of thinking about poverty is to see it as a deprivation of basic capabilities rather than as simply a lack of income.[7] In sum, poverty is a direct

---

5. Daniel G. Groody, *Globalization, Spirituality, and Justice: Navigating the Path to Peace* (Maryknoll, NY: Orbis Books, 2015), 5–6.

6. As quoted in Javier María Iguiñiz Echeverría, "The Multidimensionality of Poverty," in *The Preferential Option for the Poor beyond Theology*, ed. Daniel G. Groody and Gustavo Gutíerrez (South Bend, IN: University of Notre Dame Press, 2014), 47.

7. Amartya Sen, *Development as Freedom* (Oxford: Oxford University Press, 1999). See chapter 4 (pp. 87–110).

challenge to a person's ability to flourish; thus, any end to poverty must be measured by a person's full ability to live out her or his capabilities.

The church compels us to know our world and its inhabitants. Today, one of the signs of the times is the large number of humans who live in poverty and the scandalous gap between rich and poor. Statistics and anecdotes can form the starting point for our attempt to understand the preferential option for the poor and what it demands of our lives.

Ground Up and Filleted:
Devouring the Poor in the Old Testament

While there are many marginalized groups of people who are never given a voice within the Bible—think of women or racial minorities—such is not the case with the poor. Even a "mere glance" will show the importance of the poor in Scripture (EG 187). Marginalized, exploited, and aggrieved, they stand before the rich and the comfortable with God as their advocate, pleading for charity and justice.

The Hebrew word for the poor literally translates as "bent down" or "afflicted." This language signifies not only an economic status but a physical disposition. We need to recognize this fact, lest we run the risk of spiritualizing the Old Testament's language about the poor. As John Donahue notes, "certain contemporary usages of 'spiritual poverty,' which allow it to be used of wealthy people who are unhappy even amid prosperity, are not faithful to the biblical tradition."[8] The biblical poor are those literally deprived and afflicted, bent under the weight of injustice.

Many parts of the Old Testament would prove instructive in thinking about God's commitment to the poor. In the Exodus story, for example, God fights on behalf of the enslaved Israelites because God is a God of the oppressed. In the Wisdom literature and the Psalms, we find pithy dicta that explain God's love of the poor:

> Those who oppress the poor insult their Maker,
>   but those who are kind to the needy honor him. (Prov 14:31)

---

8. John R. Donahue, *Seek Justice That You Might Live: Reflections and Resources on the Bible and Social Justice* (New York: Paulist Press, 2014), 54–55.

> For he delivers the needy when they call,
>> the poor and those who have no helper.
> He has pity on the weak and the needy,
>> and saves the lives of the needy.
> From oppression and violence he redeems their life;
>> and precious is their blood in his sight. (Ps 72:12-14)

These two examples are just the tip of the iceberg. They demonstrate the intimate connection between God and the poor. What we do to the poor implicates our relationship with God. At the same time, God rises to protect and have mercy on the poor. God rescues and redeems this specific segment of humanity.

An important archaeological discovery in 2008 confirms that what we see in the Bible about the poor is a genuine reflection of the practice in ancient Israel. The *Khirbet Qeiyafa* ostracon—a short inscription on a piece of broken pottery—discusses the need to care for the stranger, the orphan, the widow, and the poor (see fig. 7 and 8). The inscription says to "judge" these marginalized groups, which suggests an attempt to establish legal standing for these groups in the ancient society.[9]

The strongest and most thorough advocacy for the poor in the Old Testament comes in the Prophets. The prophets Isaiah and Micah lived in Judah in the eighth century BCE. Although they were roughly contemporaneous with each other, they came from very different social locations. Isaiah was a man of the city and dealt with princes and kings, while Micah lived in the countryside.

Prophets like Isaiah and Micah can sometimes be hard to understand. Biblical scholar Walter Brueggemann provides a helpful analogy. He says that the Old Testament is like a courtroom in which we find both testimony and counter-testimony.[10] In Isaiah 3, the prophet presents his oracles with explicit courtroom imagery. God, functioning here as both lawyer and judge, stands up for the poor and accuses the rich:

---

9. There are scholarly debates about what, precisely, this ostracon says. See the discussion in Donahue, 53.

10. Walter Brueggemann, *Theology of the Old Testament: Testimony, Dispute, Advocacy* (Minneapolis: Fortress Press, 1997).

Figure 7. Khirbet Qeiyafa Ostracon. (Courtesy of Wikimedia Commons.)

Figure 8. Khirbet Qeiyafa Ostracon. (Courtesy of Wikimedia Commons.)

> The LORD rises to argue his case;
>   he stands to judge the peoples.
> The LORD enters into judgment
>   with the elders and princes of his people:
> It is you who have devoured the vineyard;
>   the spoil of the poor is in your houses.
> What do you mean by crushing my people,
>   by grinding the face of the poor? Says the Lord GOD of hosts.
>   (Isa 3:13-15)

This text from Isaiah doesn't pull any punches. The "elders and princes" have stolen the few possessions the poor might have.

Isaiah culminates his point with the image of a grinding stone, normally used for milling grain into flour. Isaiah turns this image of life and sustenance into one of torture and death. The faces of the poor are ground down to nothing beneath the weight and accumulation of the rich and powerful.

We turn now to the prophet Micah, who was from a small town called Moresheth. The prophet Micah is best known for the famous verse in 6:8: "to do justice, and to love kindness, and to walk humbly with your God." This verse, popular in email signatures, church mission statements, and drab modern liturgical songs, ought to be banned. It's a great verse, of course. But it's quite insipid and tepid when compared with the fiery rhetoric of the rest of Micah.

While Isaiah was a prophet in the city of Jerusalem, working among the kings and princes, Micah was from the countryside. This rural, outsider status might be what inspires Micah's insight into economic justice. He critiques the leaders and the kind of society they perpetuate. Images relating to economic exploitation punctuate the book. Micah refers to those who covet houses and seize them (2:2). He even critiques other prophets who see no problem with their own food and yet "declare war against those who put nothing into their mouths" (3:5). Micah depicts the entire power structure of Jerusalem as having gone off the rails:

> Hear this, you rulers of the house of Jacob
>   and chiefs of the house of Israel,
> who abhor justice
>   and pervert all equity,
> who build Zion with blood

and Jerusalem with wrong!
    Its rulers give judgment for a bribe,
        its priests teach for a price,
        its prophets give oracles for money;
    yet they lean upon the LORD and say,
        "Surely the LORD is with us!" (Mic 3:9-11)

Micah claims that the structures of power in Jerusalem are awash in money, lacking justice for the poor and vulnerable, all while claiming God is on their side.

Perhaps the most memorable image in Micah is at the beginning of chapter 3. Here, the leaders and the powerful are depicted as cannibals, devouring the flesh of the people:

Listen, you heads of Jacob
    and rulers of the house of Israel!
Should you not know justice?—
    you who hate the good and love the evil,
Who tear the skin off my people,
    and the flesh off their bones;
who eat the flesh of my people,
    flay their skin off them,
break their bones in pieces,
    and chop them up like meat in a kettle,
    like flesh in a caldron. (Mic 3:1-3)

I wish everyone who put Micah 6:8 in an Instagram post or on a bulletin cover would read these verses instead. Micah is not here to comfort the comfortable. Micah describes a deep social and structural problem. The leaders and structures exploit and devour the poor. Society is devoid of justice.

With remarkable congruence in exercising their prophetic and poetic power, both Isaiah and Micah turn the poor into food. This is the height of irony: the thing for which the poor are most desperate becomes an analogy for their destruction. Isaiah drops the faces of the poor under the very stone where the people should be pouring their grain. In Micah, the leadership butcher, fillet, and cook the poor in a pot. We need to pay attention to this graphic language, for it is part of the "enduring legacy" of the prophets, "especially in our age of colorless imagination, when suffering and poverty are reduced to statistics and euphemism." The prophets are here to "shock our imaginations."[11]

Pope Francis, in *Evangelii Gaudium*, dons the prophetic mantle in making the same rhetorical move:

> Can we continue to stand by when food is thrown away while people are starving? This is a case of inequality. Today everything comes under the laws of competition and the survival of the fittest, where the powerful feed upon the powerless. . . . Human beings are themselves considered consumer goods to be used and then discarded. . . . The excluded are not the "exploited" but the outcast, the "leftovers." (EG 53)

Francis turns the poor into the leftovers, which might be even worse than the images in Isaiah and Micah. In Francis's image, the poor are not even worth consuming. They are the thing we scrape into the garbage when we're stuffed, like the weird Jell-O dish nobody likes at Thanksgiving dinner.

Good News to the Poor: The Gospel of Luke

When people think about Jesus reaching out to and helping the poor, they are probably thinking of an example from the Gospel of Luke. Entire books have been written about how this particular gospel portrays Jesus' mission of social and economic justice. Luke's social justice agenda begins from the very start of his gospel. Mary's song, sung in response to the angel's annunciation of God's activity, reads like a thesis statement for Luke's entire gospel. This poetry, modeled on the song of Hannah in 1 Samuel 2, describes a God actively involved in human affairs:

> He has brought down the powerful from their thrones
>   and lifted up the lowly;
> he has filled the hungry with good things,
>   and sent the rich away empty. (Luke 1:52-53)

11. Donahue, *Seek Justice*, 95.

This song, known as the *Magnificat,* shows God rearranging human order based on socioeconomic distinctions. God lifts up the poor and lowly and pulls down the powerful.

Luke's emphasis on the poor continues in chapter 2, in his choosing of shepherds as those to whom the message of Jesus' birth is first announced (Luke 2:8-20). These shepherds are not cute and cuddly, put there so we can dress kids up in robes for our yearly parish pageant. In the ancient world, shepherds were untrusted and unkempt.[12] These are some of the last people on earth we might expect to be the first to hear about the birth of the king of the universe. Luke suggests that God's mission is targeted at a particular segment of the population: the poor.

We should not be surprised, then, when Jesus first speaks publicly and continues the theme. At a synagogue in his hometown, Jesus reads from Isaiah:

> The Spirit of the Lord is upon me,
>> because he has anointed me to bring good news to the poor.
>> (Luke 4:18)

This reading, Jesus says, is fulfilled among those who heard it. (In other words, it's talking about Jesus' mission.)

These programmatic images and statements from the opening chapters of Luke play out in practical ways throughout Jesus' ministry. In chapter 6, Jesus comes down from a mountain, stands among the people, and proclaims "blessed are you who are poor" (Luke 6:20). A few verses later, he asserts the opposite: "Woe to you who are rich" (6:24).

In a recent RCIA class at my parish we were praying with and discussing these verses of blessing and woe from Luke 6. A participant was adamant that Jesus meant these words to be spiritual: "There's no way they could refer to actual poverty and riches," he said. While trying to affirm this individual's struggle with what Luke says, I suggested that we can't sidestep this difficult text by spiritualizing it. Scripture gives us a spiritualized version in the Gospel of Matthew, where Jesus

---

12. See Raymond E. Brown, *The Birth of the Messiah* (Garden City, NY: Doubleday, 1977), who notes how the shepherds have overtaken the magi as the dominant Christmas symbol for the "common" person. On the contrary, the shepherds were neither "gentle or noble" but probably seen as "dishonest" (p. 420).

says "blessed are the poor *in spirit*" (Matt 5:3). Luke's version of this, however, only says "Blessed are *you who are poor*." Luke focuses on actual, physical poverty.

This RCIA participant operated with two assumptions, both of which I think many Catholics today might share. First, he assumed that God judges us according to well understood "moral issues." We like to think that God cares about whether we lie, slander, gossip, or cheat. Luke's focus is elsewhere. For Luke, the basis on which God will judge humans includes our economic status.

Second, most Catholics today assume that our faith is a spiritual and individual thing, that it is about "me and God." We try to live good lives, enriched by the sacraments, so we can get to heaven. Pope Francis points out the problem with this second assumption, saying that many today ignore the "realism of the social aspect of the Gospel" because they want a "purely spiritual Christ, without flesh and without the cross" (EG 88). Luke presents us with the truth that—like the incarnation itself, in which God became flesh—our living out the Gospel is physical and enfleshed, involving the real world.

In *Caritas et Veritate,* Benedict XVI makes a claim that might summarize the perspective in Luke, saying that "*every economic decision has a moral consequence*" (CV 37). In other words, economic decisions are moral decisions and God will use them in judging human activity. This truth ties us in knots; things are easier if we only focus on the spiritual side of faith. In the classroom, I often hear statements like "but lots of rich people are good, moral people." Or, "I know some poor people who have terrible morals." I also often hear from the pulpit that "our job is to get to heaven and take as many people with us as possible." While these statements may be true, none of them is the complete truth. The Gospel of Luke confronts us with the entire truth: that God cares both about spiritual and physical realities, that this world matters, that the living conditions of the poor matter. Salvation, to quote Gustavo Gutiérrez, "is not purely 'religious.'"[13]

Luke is perhaps most famous for his parables, many of which are unique to his gospel. These well-crafted stories also explore the economic components of the Christian faith. In chapter 16 of Luke, Jesus

---

13. Gustavo Gutiérrez, "Toward a Theology of Liberation," in *Liberation Theology: A Documentary History*, ed. Alfred T. Hennelly (Maryknoll, NY: Orbis Books, 1990), 71.

tells a story about a poor man named Lazarus. Lazarus lived at the door of an unnamed rich man, longing to fill himself with crumbs from the rich man's table. They both die. Lazarus goes to the "good place," while the rich man does not. Burning in torture, the rich man begs for a messenger to be sent to his family, so they can be warned about the eternal fate that awaits them. Abraham replies from the good place: "They have Moses and the prophets; they should listen to them" (16:29). This story reiterates the idea that our eternal destiny is at stake when we decide what to do with our money. Or, to recall the words of Benedict, *"every economic decision has a moral consequence."*

When discussing these texts in Luke with my students, one of their first reactions is to say "that's not fair." They might be right. But who are we to tell God what is fair or not fair? Are we willing to sit with poor, sore-ridden Lazarus and tell him what is fair and what is not?

Luke seems aware of the "fairness" problem. Other parables in Luke probe human objections to God's love for the poor and judgment of the rich. In Luke 15-17, Jesus spins a series of parables prompted by grumbling from the religious leaders (15:1-2). Jesus tells about a shepherd who leaves his ninety-nine sheep and seeks the one who is lost. He also uses the image of a woman who moves heaven and earth to search for one lost coin. These stories fit the depiction of God we've already seen in Luke: that God disregards those already "in the fold" and seeks out the lost and the needy. One might imagine the disgruntled protests of the ninety-nine, wondering why their shepherd is wasting his time with "that one who always wanders off." The issues raised in the parables about sheep and coins merge together into one of Luke's great masterpieces: the parable of the prodigal son (Luke 15:11-32).

Many interpretations of the prodigal son story focus on the younger brother, who receives love and mercy from his father (vv. 22-23). Once the younger son is embraced, now in drippy clothes and bling, the party starts (v. 22). Music bumping. Meat roasting. We should not forget that there is an older son involved here, too. Do you remember him? He's the dutiful oldest child who always does the right thing and never leaves. When his wasteful brother returns, the older brother is still out in the field (v. 25). As he enters the house tired, dusty, thirsty, and hungry, he hears music. One of his father's slaves explains to him what is going on (v. 26). He's a complete afterthought. We might be able to hear him say, "it's not fair." And he might be right.

According to Luke, God makes choices. God focuses divine love, grace, and attention on those who most need it. In the parable of the prodigal and his brother, the father chooses to lavish love and attention on the wasteful son, the one who doesn't deserve it. The entire situation is unfair. By focusing on the older brother, we get insight into how Luke wants his readers to think about the Gospel. It's not about "me" or "us." The question that Luke wants us to answer is this: "how will I react if I observe God being gracious to someone else?" How will I react if I observe Jesus reaching out to the poor? How will we respond? In the parable, the older brother's story is left unfinished. He states his complaint, the father responds, and the story ends before the older brother's arc is complete. Everything depends upon how the older brother will respond, but the story ends before we find out.

There can be no doubt, when looking at the biblical evidence, that God is on the side of the poor. These texts (and there are many more) are a big part of why John Paul II can so boldly claim that God's special love for the poor is a truth to which "the whole tradition of the Church bears witness" (SRS 42). These texts, when built up into the social teachings of the church, are why we use the phrase "preferential option for the poor." God chooses the poor and sheds upon them God's first grace.

The question for those of us who are not poor is this: will we learn the right lesson? Will we become aggrieved, dig in our heels, and say "that's not fair"? Or will we, to use the phrase from Óscar Romero, become "incarnate in the world of the poor"? Will we "share their fate"?

Catholic Teaching and the Modern Economy

The deep roots of God's love for the poor in the Bible mean that Catholic social teaching has had a lot to say about how Christians should think about money, possessions, and our modern economy. *Rerum Novarum*, written by Pope Leo XIII in 1891, was prompted by the industrial revolution, the increasingly contingent lives of workers, and the need for unionization. As part of his argument, he claims that the role of the state is to "promote in the highest degree the interest of the poor" (RN 26). In an era with exploding inequality and increasing corporatization of profits, Leo reminds the state of the need to look to the interests of all:

> The poor are members of the national community equally with
> the rich; they are real component parts, living parts, which make
> up, through the family, the living body; and it need hardly be said
> that they are by far the majority. It would be irrational to neglect
> one portion of the citizens and to favor another. (RN 27)

Perhaps you can hear an allusion to Paul's metaphor of the body in
Leo's words here. All, rich and poor alike, are part of the body. Thus, it
would be irrational to neglect one part, especially the most populous
part (i.e., the poor), in order to inflate a smaller portion.

Pius XI, on the fortieth anniversary of Leo's writing, introduces the
phrase "social justice" into the tradition of Catholic social teaching.
This phrase expresses the church's goals for society. His words, from
1931, remain salient today:

> Wealth, therefore, which is constantly being augmented by social
> and economic progress, must be so distributed among the various
> individuals and classes of society that the common good of all
> . . . be thereby promoted. In other words, the good of the whole
> community must be safeguarded. By these principles of social
> justice one class is forbidden to exclude the other from a share
> in the profits. (QA 57)

While Pius says that the poor should work if they are able and that they
should not demand an undue share, the bulk of the burden lies with the
rich and the powerful to make sure that all people profit from profit.

These teachings offer a sharp jab at free-market capitalism, both
in its philosophical underpinnings and its practical impacts. For example, Pius XI says that "economic affairs cannot be left to the free
play of rugged competition" (QA 88). The individualistic approach at
the root of capitalism makes it too easy to ignore the broader social
responsibilities that all individuals and leaders must have. While there
may be a proper place for a free market, rugged competition itself
"cannot be an adequate controlling principle in economic affairs"
(QA 88). Real-world evidence proves that if competition is the only
controlling force, we end up with a few winners and too many losers:
"Every sincere observer realizes that the vast differences between the
few who hold excessive wealth and the many who live in destitution
constitute a grave evil in modern society" (QA 58). Capitalism alone,

both in philosophy and in practicality, does not create the conditions for the socially just society that God desires.

The church's critique of capitalism and call for distribution oriented toward the common good does not mean the church is in favor of socialism. The church critiques socialism as well. In the first half of the twentieth century, when these teachings were being formulated, socialism was a quickly-changing ideology taking many different forms throughout the world. Pius himself notes that there are many aspects of it on which the church must take a "wait and see" approach to see if they bear some fruit on behalf of social justice. Pius, however, does critique the core ideology of socialism as essentially unchristian. It is based on a utilitarian ideology, one in which work and individualism must be "subordinated and even sacrificed to the exigencies of efficient production" (QA 119). The way socialism subordinates individuality to the needs of the state and production can lead to a loss in human dignity.

Several years ago, one of my kids had a friend whose dad drove a huge SUV with the vanity license plate: "CPTLSM." I asked my son about it and he responded: "Well, I guess he's really trying to say that he doesn't like socialism." Even a ten-year-old perceives the way socialism and capitalism are played off each other in modern-day American discourse. Given the geopolitical conflicts of the Unites States over the last seventy years, many of which had stopping socialism as part of their justification, we now see the world through a bifurcated "capitalism vs. socialism" framework. I don't think it is a stretch to say that many Christians today see their faith in God and their faith in capitalism as almost one and the same. I know, from conversation, that this was certainly the case for my friend with the CPTLSM license plate.

The truths from Scripture and Catholic social teaching will not fit into this dualistic framework. The church's social doctrine "adopts a critical attitude toward both liberal capitalism and Marxist collectivism" (SRS 21). Scripture and church teaching speak prophetically, critiquing the problems of our world and offering moral frameworks for how to make things better.

There is no doubt, however, that the foundational principles of capitalism, based on self-interest, are at odds with the goals of Catholic social teaching, which are solidarity, reciprocity, and gratuitousness. Capitalism makes humans into *Homo economicus*, a wrongheaded identity that suggests that the "good of the person is synonymous with the satisfaction of subjective materials preferences."[14] In other words, capitalism turns us into nothing other than economic beings, our function in the world reduced to desire and consumption.

Capitalism has brought good things. A thoughtful introduction of a market-based economy has increased living conditions in many parts of the world.[15] These realities, however, should not lead to blind trust in a market system. We must avoid a "crude and naive trust in the goodness of those wielding economic power and in the sacralized workings of the prevailing economic system" (EG 54). Because we have not adopted a critical stance toward capitalism, we have become "enchanted" by it. It forms our moral imagination and provides our spiritual formation.[16]

While we put our faith in the capitalist system, Pope Francis says, the excluded "are still waiting" (EG 54). So, while the church does not propose a specific economic system or theory, it offers principles and guidelines for how to judge the success of a modern economy. Because of God's preference for the poor, and the goal of a socially just society, we can see that our modern system of rugged competition only works for a few.

John Paul II and "Superdevelopment"

The church's social documents are a living, developing body of teachings, as Benedict XVI says, *"consistent and at the same time ever new"* (CV 12). As these teachings developed over time, and the church meditated on the social teaching and its implications, we see a growing depth of insight into the causes of the social problems of our world. John Paul II is a perfect example of this new depth. His background and experiences, having lived through the Second World War and seen up close the world of national socialism and Soviet communism

14. Anthony Annett, *Cathonomics: How Catholic Tradition Can Create a More Just Economy* (Washington, DC: Georgetown University Press, 2022), 73.

15. See, for example, some of the approaches outlined by Jeffrey D. Sachs, *The End of Poverty: Economic Possibilities for Our Time* (New York: Penguin, 2006). And note the statistics in George Enderle, "The Option for the Poor and Business Ethics," in *Preferential Option for the Poor beyond Theology*, ed. Groody and Gutíerrez.

16. Eugene McCarraher, "Enchanted Capitalism," *Plough Quarterly* 36 (2023): 40.

in his native Poland, gives him unique insight into the dynamics of the economy in the twentieth century and beyond.

John Paul II notes the serious problems of "underdevelopment" in our world. Due to various aspects of poverty, the poor throughout the world find it impossible to live out their authentic human flourishing. He notes that there is a "well-founded anxiety for the fate of humanity" based in part on the "miseries of underdevelopment" (SRS 27). Humanity saw many great developments during John Paul's lifetime (1920–2005). These developments, however, need to be guided by "a moral understanding and by an orientation toward the true good of the human race." Without an orientation to the common good, development ironically turns against humans and can cause oppression, especially of the poor.

Just as concerning as underdevelopment, John Paul says, is a form of "superdevelopment." The new shiny objects served to us by our economy are "inadmissible" because they are contrary to what is proper to human happiness. John Paul II, writing in 1987, could just as easily be describing our world, decades later:

> This superdevelopment, which consists in an *excessive* availability of every kind of material goods for the benefit of certain social groups, easily makes people slaves of "possession" and immediate gratification, with no other horizon than the multiplication of continual replacement of the things already owned with others still better. This is the so-called civilization of "consumption" or "consumerism," which involves so much "throwing-away" and "waste." An object already owned but now superseded by something better is discarded, with no thought of its possible lasting value in itself, nor of some other human being who is poorer. (SRS 28)

I'm not sure that more prophetic words have been written or spoken in the last 50 years. John Paul could be describing Amazon two-day delivery or DoorDash. When the iPhone starts to feel dull, we supplement it with a watch. When Facebook runs dry, we slurp up TikTok. We feed capitalism with no thought for its impact on the poor; "the culture of prosperity deadens us" (EG 54). *"Every economic decision has a moral consequence"* (CV 37).

John Paul takes these observations about our world and translates them into concrete actions based upon what he calls the *"love of preference* for the poor"* (SRS 42). This is a *"special form* of primacy" that tells us something about God, but also about our own *"social responsibilities* and hence to our manner of living" (SRS 42). If we ignore our duties, what we do with our ownership and goods, we run the risk of "becoming like the 'rich man' who pretended not to know the beggar Lazarus lying at his gate" (SRS 42). John Paul refers to the poor as the "Lord's poor," based upon the biblical texts we explored above. This group must be a "motivating concern" translated "at all levels into concrete actions" (SRS 43).

John Paul II orients his call for concrete actions to a global scale. He talks about international trade; world monetary and financial systems; self-affirmation within developing nations; literacy and education; food production; and the importance of participatory political institutions. It's overwhelming. This does not mean, however, that we should not start to try to make changes.

In his writing to commemorate the hundredth anniversary of Leo's original *Rerum Novarum*, John Paul II summarizes all we've been discussing here quite well, particularly emphasizing the importance of the option for the poor, its deep structural components, and the need for all humans to live differently:

> Love for others, and in the first place love for the poor, in whom the church sees Christ himself [see Matthew 25], is made concrete in the promotion of justice. Justice will never be fully attained unless people see in the poor person, who is asking for help in order to survive, not an annoyance or a burden, but an opportunity for showing kindness and a chance of greater enrichment. Only such an awareness can give the courage needed to face the risk and the change involved in every authentic attempt to come to the aid of another. It is not merely a matter of "giving from one's surplus," but of helping entire peoples which are presently excluded or marginalized to enter into the sphere of economic and human development. For this to happen, it is not enough to draw on the surplus goods which in fact our world abundantly produces; it requires above all a change of lifestyles, of models of production and consumption, and of the established structures of power which today govern societies. (CA 58)

In other words, to live out the Gospel in accord with the preferential option for the poor, we need an entirely new world.

Revolution of Tenderness

Having seen the strong words from Scripture and tradition regarding the poor, we can understand what Peter Maurin meant when he said that we should "blow the dynamite of the church." The church's teaching on economic matters is explosive. Both the Bible and the church's social teachings envision and advocate for an entirely new way of living, one that is not based on greed, accumulation, and chasing after the shiny new object. These teachings ask of us two essential things: first, that we recognize and seek to end structures in our world that perpetuate poverty. Second, that every economic decision we make in our own lives be considered in light of the poor. When we decide to upgrade our phone, get a bigger boat, fly first class, or buy a Lexus, our relationship with God is implicated.

These teachings are hard; nobody wants to hear or think about them. The problems of poverty in our world are so big and entangled that they seem daunting. Much of Catholic social teaching focuses on the big, global components of poverty and its implications. What is the average person to do?

We return to Óscar Romero, whose words we quoted toward the beginning of this chapter. Romero spent much of his life as a shy academic. Eventually he became bishop in El Salvador, which caused him to have a deep encounter with the plight of his people that changed his life. He spent his last years as an activist and advocate for the liberation of the poor in his native country. He was changed by this encounter. His experience led him to lay out the path for all Christians, who need to "share the fate" of the poor and "become incarnate in their world."

Romero takes a major cue for his understanding of faith from the incarnation of Jesus. Jesus did not come to earth among the rich. The incarnation—God becoming flesh—happened in a specific and intentional way:

> I am not speaking of a universal incarnation. This is impossible.
> I am speaking of an incarnation that is preferential and partial:
> incarnation in the world of the poor. . . . The world of the poor,

with its very concrete social and political characteristics, teaches us where the church can incarnate itself in such a way that it will avoid the false universalism that inclines the church to associate itself with the powerful.[17]

Jesus' poor birth certifies divine intention; God did this on purpose. Because Jesus himself became poor, so must each individual and the whole church become incarnate in the world of the poor.

These words from Romero are the leading edge of what Scripture and tradition would demand of our lives. We must get involved in the lives of the poor. God, in Jesus, humbled the divine nature to be specifically with the poor. This act of self-giving demands everything of us as well. Romero, in his last homily, ties this need for being with the poor to our reception of the Eucharist: "May this body immolated and this blood sacrificed for humans nourish us also, so that we may give our body and our blood to suffering and to pain—like Christ, not for self, but to impart notions of justice and peace to our people."[18]

If Romero gives us the direction our lives need to take—being incarnate in the world of the poor—what does that look like in a practical way? Pope Francis can help us answer this question. He provides language and ideas for practical application of what Scripture and the church's social teachings say about the poor. We can summarize what Francis calls for in one word: "encounter."[19] What does encounter look like?

> The Gospel tells us constantly to run the risk of a face-to-face encounter with others, with their physical presence which challenges us, with their pain and their pleas, with their joy which infects us in our close and continuous interaction. True faith in the incarnate Son of God is inseparable from self-giving, from membership in community, from service, from reconciliation with others. The Son of God, by becoming flesh, summoned us to the revolution of tenderness. (EG 88)

17. Romero, "Political Dimension of the Faith," 299.

18. Romero, "Last Homily," in *Liberation Theology: A Documentary History*, ed. Alfred T. Hennelly (Maryknoll, NY: Orbis Books, 1990), 306.

19. For a helpful exploration of the concept of encounter, see Marcus Mescher, *The Ethics of Encounter: Christian Neighbor Love as a Practice of Solidarity* (Maryknoll, NY: Orbis, 2020).

There is only one way to enact the revolution of tenderness: be involved in the life of a poor person. Get to know them. Have a genuine encounter. Francis's insight here is born of his own decades of work with the poor in Buenos Aires. Genuine encounter is challenging. We encounter pain, pleading, and even physical repulsion. These are the things we must risk in order to get involved in the lives of others. Too many Catholics today think their work for the poor can begin and end with advocacy and charity. We are called to be and do more, we are called to become incarnate in their world.

In 2016, when most people seemed to think a Facebook post was enough to stop President Trump's immigration ban, I decided to call the refugee resettlement organization, World Relief, to see how I could help. They put me in contact with a recent refugee from Myanmar. He had been in a terrible industrial accident and much of his face and body was covered with burns. As a result, he is blind in one eye and has profound hearing loss. Ten years after the accident, skin grafts and other reconstructive surgeries continue. I help him shop. I help him get his bike fixed. I have spread salve on his wounds after surgery. I shared his grief when his father, back in Myanmar, died of COVID. I listened to his anxiety during the military coup in his homeland in 2021. While our relationship started somewhat transactionally—mostly me helping him with things—over time, he has become my friend. He listened and laughed with me when one of my kids got his driver's license and immediately hit a parked car. He is one of the few people I know who understands my own anxiety when I have to see the doctor. He teases me because I don't clean the garbage out of the front seat of my car. He helps me find good buys at the Asian grocery store.

I offer this friendship as an example of encounter. There is no agenda. I try not to think of it as charity. Pope Francis says that this type of encounter is "essential" even if it appears "to bring us no tangible and immediate benefits" (EG 210). While it is not always easy, and often inconvenient, it is one attempt to live out what the church calls for in the preferential option for the poor. I like to think that, even in a small way, this encounter helps me demonstrate my belief in the Son of God and how his incarnation is inseparable from self-giving. By coming close, God modeled for us the need to become close to others, to risk the "revolution of tenderness" (EG 88).

We all have room for at least one ongoing encounter in our lives. Do you know at least one homeless person by name? Have you ever had a conversation with someone who was desperately poor? While the problems of global poverty seem daunting, John Paul II says that we must start small: "Justice will never be fully attained unless people see in the poor person, who is asking for help in order to survive, not an annoyance or a burden, but an opportunity for showing kindness and a chance for greater enrichment" (CA 58).

There are two impediments to this type of encounter. The first impediment is that most people are ignorant about what Scripture and the church teach concerning the place of the poor in the heart of God. The second impediment is selfishness. Pope Francis warns against "an overbearing need to guard" our free time, "as if the task of evangelization was a dangerous poison rather than a joyful response to God's love which summons us to mission" (EG 81). We need to live out the connection between our faith and the poor, and we need to stop guarding our time as if it actually belonged to us.

The call to Christians to evangelize the world, in all times and places, does not abate. Where are we to go? How do we evangelize? What are we supposed to do? Pope Francis gives an answer: "When we read the Gospel we find a clear indication: [we should go] not so much [to] our friends and wealthy neighbors, but above all [to] the poor and the sick, those who are usually despised and overlooked." He continues:

> There can be no room for doubt or for explanations which weaken so clear a message. Today and always, "the poor are the privileged recipients of the Gospel." . . . We have to state, without mincing words, that there is an inseparable bond between our faith and the poor. May we never abandon them. (EG 48)

While we seek mirth and beauty, there are frail forms fainting at our door. We must get involved in their lives, become incarnate in their world, and share their fate. God chooses the poor, and so must we.

chapter 5

"Truly Act Justly with One Another"

Becoming Common Gooders

O Lord, my heart is not proud
    nor my look haughty;
I do not aspire to great things
    or to what is beyond me;
but I have taught myself to be contented.

             —Psalm 131:1-2, JPS

Every year my extended family rents a few rustic cabins on the shore of Lake Superior. As four or five family units come together, it can be difficult to figure out what to do each day. Some want to hike. Some want to shop. Some want to swim. Some want to lay on the rocks. Some just want cocktails.

This anecdote might get us thinking about the common good. How do disparate constituencies come together to decide what is "good"? How can something with such a subjective definition ever become shared, truly "common" among all? The phrase "common good" gets used a lot, but always comes with this significant problem. How do we define it? What *is* the common good?

When I ask my students how they would define the common good, they often come up with what is called a "utilitarian" definition: whatever does the most good, for the most people, most of the time. This definition intuitively makes sense: our society should aim for a broad middle path that works for most people most of the time.

This utilitarian definition has two problems. First, it requires very little sacrifice from members of society. A vague sense that "everything is okay" is often enough to get us off the hook from thinking about the plight and suffering of people, not only in our own communities, but also around the planet (not to mention the suffering of the planet itself).

Second, the utilitarian definition of the common good tends toward equilibrium. If most people are okay most of the time, we never work to eliminate problems facing those on the margins. If we're not careful, we can end up reinforcing "normative and practical-systemic forms of inherited power."[1] In other words, if those defining and working toward the common good are those who also wield political and economic power, their definitions and programs might only serve to reinforce their own power. Seeking the common good, ironically, could be a barrier to the change we need in the world.

We have quite a task ahead of us in this chapter! First, I want to suggest that we get rid of the idea of "defining" the common good. The common good is not about a definition, but a way of living. What actually makes it difficult is not its definition, but what it requires of us. As the church's compendium of social teaching makes clear, the common good "is very difficult to attain because it requires the constant ability and effort to seek the good of others as though it were one's own good" (CSDC 167). The only way to attain the common good is by making self-sacrificial choices at every turn of life.

Remember Jesus' parable about the vineyard workers? A landowner sends people out to work at 9 in the morning, noon, 3 in the afternoon, and 5 in the evening. They all got paid the same daily wage. Those who toiled all day are understandably disgruntled: "These last worked only one hour, and you have made them equal to us who have borne the burden of the day and the scorching heat" (Matt 20:12). The landowner's reply is rather simple: I can do whatever I want to do with my money. Jesus summarizes the parable by saying: "the last will be first, and the first will be last" (Matt 20:16).

---

1. Anna Rowlands, *Toward a Politics of Communion: Catholic Social Teaching in Dark Times* (London: T&T Clark, 2021), 113.

This parable can help us start to think about how Scripture and tradition define the common good. The common good is not so much a flattening but a reversal. It is not a sharing equally among all, but a flipping of the social order. To achieve the common good, we must work at every moment, both as individuals and as a society, to prioritize those who come in last.

In this chapter, we will focus on two individuals from Scripture who can help give practical examples of how to think about the common good. The first is Jeremiah, a prophet from the sixth century BCE. He preaches to Judah at a time when God does not think the people and its leadership have properly created a world that reflects the common good. The second example takes us into the home of a slaveowner in Colossae named Philemon. In this situation, Paul, fueled by his understanding of the Gospel, asks Philemon to seek the good of the other in a very awkward situation.

Jeremiah: Live Justly with One Another

Jeremiah knew tragedy. He lived through the Babylonian exile, a cataclysm that provoked a crisis for the Jewish people. The sacking of Jerusalem called into question their relationship with God, the promises God had made, and pressed them to consider the reasons for undeserved suffering. In the midst of this upheaval, the book of Jeremiah offers narratives and poetic oracles attempting to make sense of their shattered community.

Jeremiah's story starts off great. One of the most famous verses of the Old Testament comes to Jeremiah from God:

> Before I formed you in the womb I knew you,
> and before you were born I consecrated you;
> I appointed you a prophet to the nations. (Jer 1:5)

This all sounds fine and dandy, until we come to learn what this call means for Jeremiah. It means ridicule, hatred, and imprisonment by his own people because they don't like God's message. God appoints Jeremiah to "pluck up and to pull down, to destroy and to overthrow" (Jer 1:10). Although Jeremiah's call gets put on bumper stickers and inspirational posters—who wouldn't like the idea of God choosing us before birth?—it quickly becomes clear that Jeremiah wants no part of being chosen by God.

At the beginning of chapter 7, God warns the people that they should "amend" their ways. One of God's main accusations is idolatry; the people are worshipping foreign gods. Because of their idolatry, God has abandoned the temple (7:4). But God quickly clarifies the conditions under which God will return to them: "If you truly act justly one with another, if you do not oppress the alien, the orphan, and the widow, or shed innocent blood in this place, and if you do not go after other gods to your own hurt, then I will dwell with you in this place" (Jer 7:5-7). God's presence in the temple is conditional on their ability to build a certain type of society, one in which they worship God and they "truly act justly with one another."

One of the things Jeremiah helps us understand is that the problems of idolatry and justice are linked together. In Jeremiah, we could say that a lack of justice in society is a form of idolatry itself. Building a society without justice proves that one does not authentically know or worship God. A world with social stratification, with "haves" and "have-nots," is akin to turning your back on the God of Israel.

God proclaims that there will be no divine protection from the threats of Babylon because of their social problems:

> Woe to him who builds his house by unrighteousness,
>   and his upper rooms by injustice;
> who makes his neighbors work for nothing,
>   and does not give them their wages. (Jer 22:13)

God finds it ridiculous to build with luxury in order to try to prove your worth. Opulence does not make one great. Past leaders knew how to act with justice and things went well because they "judged the cause of the poor and needy" (22:16). In Jeremiah's day, however, they have lost their bearing. The problem, God says, is that:

> your eyes and heart
>   are only on your dishonest gain,
> for shedding innocent blood,
>   and for practicing oppression and violence. (Jer 22:17)

The sins of the nation cause God to abandon them. God says that there will be no protection for the people against the advance of Nebuchadrezzar of Babylon (21:1-10). God compares divine action to a potter, who can imprint any design on the clay: "Look, I am a potter shaping evil against you and devising a plan against you. Turn now, all of you from your evil way, and amend your ways and your doings" (18:11).

The personal consequences for Jeremiah because of his message from God, delivered to the people, are horrible. He suffers rejection and imprisonment in a cistern (chaps. 37–38). The people, and especially the leadership in Jerusalem, understandably don't like the message that God has abandoned them because they don't seek the common good.

With his life in shambles, Jeremiah claims to have been manipulated by God:

> You duped me, O Lord, and I let myself be duped;
> you were too strong for me, and you triumphed.
> All the day I am an object of laughter;
> everyone mocks me. (Jer 20:7 NAB)

Apparently, the translators of the New American Bible did not like the idea of God duping anyone, let alone Jeremiah. Their revised edition in 2010 (NABRE) changed the word "duped" to "seduced." "Duped" better captures Jeremiah's experience. The excitement and privilege Jeremiah feels when God chooses him (chap. 1) turns out to be a ruse. The practical impact for Jeremiah is mockery and rejection. In the end, Jeremiah says that he wishes God had killed him in the womb, before he was born, rather than have to bear the calumnies against him (Jer 20:14-18).

The book of Jeremiah never uses the phrase "the common good." Yet its poetry and prose are oriented towards just that. While we today might tie ourselves in knots trying to define the "common good," Jeremiah offers instead a course of action: "truly act justly with one another." This is no definition at all; it is a way of living. Rather than defining the common good, Jeremiah calls us to be "common gooders."

Jeremiah and the Common Good in Catholic Social Teaching

In Jeremiah, the focus is on how individual actions in society have built injustice; the rich and the rulers act with no regard for the common good. When the prophet critiques the nation for dishonest gain, for shedding innocent blood, and for oppressing the alien, the orphan, and the widow, he's talking about an entire system that has lost sight of God's desires. These social problems are built up from the choices and actions of individuals, but Jeremiah's main focus is at the corporate, social, and structural level. When Catholic social teaching discusses the common good, it also often focuses on the big picture: the responsibility of leaders, governments, and society as a whole to build the right kind of society.

One text that discusses the common good at some length is *Mater et Magistra*, written by John XXIII in 1961. The state, John says, has the purpose of "the realization of the common good in the temporal order" (MM 20).[2] In order to accomplish this, the state must look out for the needs of those who are weaker, especially workers, women, and children. All labor must be oriented towards justice and equity. When thinking about work, society should never lose sight of the "dignity of the human being," for it must be respected both in body and in spirit (MM 21).

The way *Mater et Magistra* describes the common good comports perfectly with what we saw in Jeremiah. Jeremiah even seems to share the concern about worker exploitation when he mentions neighbors who "work for nothing" and people who do not give just wages (22:13). The nation's lack of justice for the most vulnerable brings God's abandonment and judgment.

In the United States today, we have a mixed track record in orienting our society toward the common good. There are many things on the positive side of the ledger. We have social programs like Social Security, Medicare and Medicaid, and welfare systems that help provide for those in need. Such programs intend to create a baseline of conditions for all people, and the church's teaching would support them.

On the other hand, much of our political rhetoric focuses on the "middle class." While this makes sense intuitively, it is essentially asking us to make a big middle, disregarding the top and the bottom. What we see in Jeremiah and in Catholic social teaching is the opposite. Our social aims should not just be a flattening, but should instead

2. Pope John XXIII, *Mater et Magistra*, May 15, 1961, in *Catholic Social Thought: Encyclicals and Documents from Pope Leo XIII to Pope Francis*, 3rd ed., ed. David J. O'Brien and Thomas A. Shannon (Maryknoll, NY: Orbis Books, 2016).

focus on the margins—both the bottom and the top—in order to create conditions in which all can flourish. Those at the top—those with more—have a greater responsibility to share their goods with those who are in need. Pope John states something similar in *Pacem in Terris*, that the common good should attend to the "less fortunate member of the community, since they are less able to defend their rights and to assert their legitimate claims" (PT 56).

Often left out of these conversations are corporations. We tend to judge them by profit margin alone; the common good is rarely, if ever, a factor in evaluating business performance. If a company's sole goal is profit, if it is beholden only to its shareholders and bottom line, we have no hope of ever achieving the common good. On the contrary, as John Paul II says, profitability should not be "the only indicator of a firm's condition" (CA 35). Corporate enterprises should "perform their work not merely with the objective of deriving an income, but also of carrying out the role assigned them and of performing a service that results in benefit to others" (MM 92). In our business-dominated society, we find a "failure of moral imagination" because we don't stop to ask "whether any of the stuff that we produced actually contributed to human flourishing."[3]

Corporations also are responsible for the dignity of work. John XXIII points out the "profound sadness" he feels when observing that workers in many nations "and in whole continents, receive too small a return from their labor" (MM 68). These individuals and groups are forced to "live in conditions completely out of accord with human dignity" (MM 68). There is plenty of blame to go around for these terrible conditions. Certainly, every consumer must think critically about her or his own purchasing habits. Governments also need to think about those on the margins when making policy decisions.

While *Mater et Magistra* has many scattered, if undeveloped, references to Scripture, none of them are to the book of Jeremiah. I'm not surprised, but I'm also disappointed. The voice of God that Jeremiah proclaimed to Jerusalem over 2,500 years ago bears a strong resemblance to how Catholic social teaching talks about the common good. At every turn societies must create conditions for the authentic

---

3. Eugene McCarraher, "Enchanted Capitalism," *Plough Quarterly* 36 (2023): 38.

flourishing and development of the weakest members of society. When God, through Jeremiah, proclaims "truly act justly with one another," we have our orders to implement just conditions in all layers of society, to engage in common gooding.

Philemon's Dilemma

Every August our local symphony presents a "pops" concert in downtown Davenport, Iowa. It's one of the great events of the year. Thousands of people flock to the banks of the Mississippi River, ply themselves with fancy food and drink, and sing along and dance to the music of famous pop artists, such as Elton John, the Beatles, or Queen. Most people arrive early and stake out a space where their group will hang out. This past summer, there were some issues. A group right in front of my family had arrived extremely early to get prime territory, a lot more than they needed. As people continued to arrive, spaces tightened, and people started snipping at this group and their excessive sward. Given the current state of humanity, you can probably guess where this is heading. Snide comments turned into yelling. I almost called 911 when a fight was imminent.

What we explored above in Jeremiah and *Mater et Magistra* focused on the big picture, the broad ways society and businesses should work for the common good. But our daily lives also present us with opportunities to live out the common good. Jeremiah's definition, that we should "truly act justly with one another," takes on new resonance in individual and interpersonal situations. I doubt that most people are thinking about the common good when they try to reserve a patch of grass for an outdoor concert. But they should be. There is only one way to put Jeremiah's definition into practice. To "live justly with one another" means that we must always choose the good of the other before choosing our own good. Simple to say; hard to do.

I want to demonstrate an interpersonal sense of the common good in a concrete way by turning to Paul's underutilized letter to Philemon. You may not have heard much about this letter. It is one of my favorites because it demonstrates how to live out the Gospel—how to be like Jesus—in the midst of a very specific, interpersonal conflict. Paul provides a path that can give us some ways to think about how to be common gooders in our everyday lives.

My students are always happy when I assign Paul's letter to Philemon because it is by far Paul's shortest. In only twenty-five verses we glimpse a Netflix-worthy drama. I suggest you go read it right now.

Scene:

> The Lycus valley (in western central Türkiye). A network of churches in three Greco-Roman cities: Hierapolis, Laodicea, and Colossae (see Colossians 4:12-13). (See fig. 9)

Figure 9. Archaeological remains of a house church in Laodicea, with Hierapolis and Colossae in the distance, three cities in an early Christian network. (Author's photo.)

Dramatis Personae:

> Paul: An apostle of Jesus Christ, writing from prison in Ephesus (about 120 miles to the east). Likely founder of the churches in the Lycus Valley. Father in faith to Philemon and his household.

> Philemon: A wealthy man who owns slaves and lives in a large home. A convert to the church. Hosts a church community in his home, probably in Colossae.

> Onesimus: A slave, owned by Philemon, who has run away. He may have stolen property from Philemon as well. He was close to Paul and has run to him for help.

Plot:

> Onesimus carries a letter, written by Paul, to be delivered to his owner, Philemon. In the letter, Paul hopes to convince Philemon not to punish his slave, to take him back, and to see him in a new way. The letter is addressed not only to Philemon, but to the whole church who meets in his house.

Scene:

> After Onesimus delivers the letter, Philemon reads it in front of the church gathered in his home.

Imagine Philemon: Master of his domain. Owner of slaves. A mover and a shaker. Somebody who matters and gets things done. He gives orders and they are followed. He makes money hand over fist, perhaps in the textile business, for which the Lycus valley was famous. He is in control, lines of power well demarcated.

He has been changed, however, by Paul's preaching of the Gospel. We don't know what drew him to it, but he was drawn. He owes Paul his very life (Phlm 19). Even after he joins the church, however, he keeps his status. A wealthy man with a house large enough to host a church gathering, he is still at the top, the power structures still in place.

But there's a bur under his saddle, a fleck of sand in his eye. Onesimus, his trusted slave, has stolen something from him and run off to Paul. This sticks in Philemon's craw because it doesn't fit; it is not how things are supposed to work. Slaves are supposed to obey. The punishments Philemon has the right to inflict, if and when Onesimus were ever to return, could include death.

Imagine Onesimus. He ran away from his owner to Paul. He wanted to stay with Paul, his new friend. But Paul sends him back with a letter, its contents unknown. Onesimus holds it up to the Mediterranean sun, trying to read it without breaking the seal.[4] He arrives tired and

---

4. My wife, inconveniently, asked me if Onesimus would have been able to read. Given what we know of the low literacy rates in the ancient world, a slave like Onesimus was unlikely to be able to read. But this is a dramatic retelling, so let's just go with it.

dusty from the long journey from Ephesus back to Colossae (see fig. 10). Imagine his anxiety. All that stands between Onesimus and death is a thin piece of parchment. On it, a personal message from Paul, a spiritual father to both owner and slave. A few strokes of a quill are all that's left to stop the stroke from a sword.

Figure 10. Roman-era street in Laodicea. Onesimus may have walked this very street on his way from Ephesus back to Colossae. (Author's photo.)

As Philemon reads the letter, addressed not only to him, but also to Apphia, Archippus, and the entire church that gathers in his house, the blood drains from his face. All eyes blink his direction, all breath baited, wondering where this is going.

Paul proceeds through a litany of rhetorical moves to try to get Philemon, and all those with him, on his side: "I'm an old man, and suffering here in prison." "I really want this situation to be resolved on the basis of love." "I could command you to obey me, but I'd rather you do it out of love."

Paul lays it on thick—not without warrant—that he is old, imprisoned, and needs sympathy. Philemon rolls his eyes. He's being manipulated. Paul is playing to the crowd. It's that awkward moment when someone tries to take advantage of their disadvantages.

Sympathy alone, however, can't fix the problem. Forcing obedience will not solve the deep rift between Philemon and Onesimus. If Philemon spares Onesimus's life, yet still bears bitterness towards him in his heart, the rift remains.

Philemon may have been prepared for Paul to intervene. He may have even steeled himself to have to spare Onesimus's life. Maybe he even planned on making a show of his forbearance and forgiveness against this wretched slave. Nothing could have prepared him, however, for what Paul requires.

Paul asks for something deeper and more substantial than forgiveness. Paul's solution is for Philemon to see Onesimus differently. Paul asks Philemon to treat Onesimus as one who has been transformed:

> Perhaps this is the reason he was separated from you for a while, so that you might have him back forever, no longer as a slave but more than a slave, a beloved brother—especially to me but how much more to you, both in the flesh and in the Lord. (Phlm 15-16)

If you listen, you can hear Philemon's world crumbling. The foundation of his power and control has been obliterated. The structure that animates his actions no longer exists. Paul asks Philemon to see Onesimus no longer as a possession but as a brother; with one stroke of the pen, the world has changed.

Roman-era slaves felt ownership in their bodies. Not only was their physical well-being threatened, but they also were marked with collars and restraints (see fig. 11). In this context, Paul's words stand out all the more starkly. Paul normally talks about "the flesh" as something negative. He often contrasts the flesh (bad) with the spirit (good) (see Romans 8:1-11). So, when Paul tells Philemon to take back Onesimus "both in the flesh and in the Lord," he makes it clear that the physical and spiritual go together. Philemon can't claim to be "in the Lord" while ignoring Onesimus's literal flesh. There must be a physical reality to reflect the spiritual belonging. Philemon must create the conditions for Onesimus's good in a physical way.

Figure 11. Roman-era slave collar. (Courtesy Wikimedia Commons.)

Philemon's problem, throughout this whole scenario, was that he was putting himself at the center. He asked: what are my rights? What do I deserve? How do I retain power? How do I preserve my own status? Onesimus's recalcitrance, to Philemon, was an impediment. Paul requires him, instead, to see Onesimus as an opportunity to put on Christ (Rom 13:4), humble himself (Phil 2), and seek the good of the other. Paul asks of Philemon the same thing he asked of the Corinthians: "do not seek your own advantage, but that of the other" (1 Cor 10:24).

As we noted above, the church's teaching on the common good generally focuses on the social and corporate level—asking leaders and rulers to think about the good of all, not just some. At some point, however, we need to make this more granular, so that individuals can think about what it means practically in their everyday lives. Indeed, these two things need to work closely together. The corporate level requires policies and procedures that care for the common good. But that's the easy part. It is much harder, I would argue, at the personal level. The common good is "very difficult to attain because it requires the constant ability and effort to seek the good of others as though it were one's own good" (CSDC 167). As Anna Rowlands says more succinctly, "the common good is held in the relationship between people."[5]

On Pope Francis's trip to Mongolia in September 2023, he stopped to visit with charity workers, who were opening a facility called the House of Mercy, where the homeless and destitute can find food, shelter, and other services. In his brief remarks, Francis ended by saying, "in a word, to truly do good, goodness of heart is essential: a commitment to seeking what is best for others."[6] These simple words sum up the interpersonal way to think about the common good. It is held in the relationship between people.

We do not have a letter from Philemon to Paul; his response to Paul is lost to history. What is clear, however, is what the Gospel requires: a Christlike love and sacrifice on behalf of the other. This overlooked letter from the Lycus valley gives us the perfect example of what it means to be a common gooder.

Who Speaks for the Trees?

Remember *The Lorax*? (The book, not the terrible movie with too many famous voice actors.) A funny creature pops from the stump of a felled tree and says, "I'm the Lorax. I speak for the trees." This children's book expressed the disconnect between human action and the good of the natural world. The Lorax channels creation, speaking up for that which has no voice. It presents environmental destruction as

5. Rowlands, *Towards a Politics of Communion*, 130.
6. "Apostolic Journey of the Holy Father Francis in Mongolia," https://press.vatican.va/content/salastampa/en/bollettino/pubblico/2023/09/04/230904b.html.

a problem resulting from human power and achievement. The Brown Bar-ba-loots, the Swomee-Swans, and the Humming-Fish bear the brunt of greed and pollution. This book's emotional power derives from its personification of nature, helping us see how we ignore the good of all creatures. *The Lorax* suggests that we should care about these creatures and their ability to live and flourish.

If we think we can care about the common good without also thinking about our common home, we fool ourselves. The hurdles to achieving the common good we explored above—greed, selfishness, love of power, and injustice—are the very things causing our current environmental crisis.

As a species, we treat the natural world the way Philemon wanted to treat Onesimus—as an object. Like the corrupt leadership in Jeremiah's day, this objectification leads to an unjust world—both for the earth and the poor. Pope Francis points out in *Laudate Deum* that we treat the goods of the earth as a resource at our disposal: "Everything that exists ceases to be a gift for which we should be thankful, esteem and cherish, and instead becomes a slave, prey to any whim of the human mind and its capacities" (LD 22).[7] If the common good, therefore, is always to seek the good of the other, the conclusion should be quite simple: our relationship with the earth might be the most important aspect of the common good. It is the relationship from which all others flow and are rendered.

The beginnings of the church's social teachings on the environment almost sound like the popes were reading *The Lorax*. John Paul II ties the ecological problems in our world to the problem of consumerism: "In his desire to have and to enjoy rather than to be and to grow, man consumes the resources of the earth and his own life in an excessive and disordered way" (CA 37). At the root of our environmental problems, John Paul says, is an "anthropological error," by which he means disordered human hearts who think it is our job to control, dominate, and consume. Blinded by our own sense of self-worth and our abilities—look what we can do!—we forget the divine origin of all we have.

---

7. Pope Francis, *Laudate Deum*, Apostolic Exhortation on the Occasion of the Fifth Centenary of the Death of St. Francis of Assisi, https://www.vatican.va/content/francesco/en/apost_exhortations/documents/20231004-laudate-deum.html.

John Paul II is essentially saying that our relationship with the natural world is out of whack. We see it as something to consume and dominate. What we lack is the "disinterested, unselfish and aesthetic attitude that is born of wonder in the presence of being and of the beauty which enables one to see in visible things the message of the invisible God who created them" (CA 37). John Paul here offers a call to approach the natural world with an attitude of selflessness and wonder.

Pope Benedict XVI expands on this problem in his social encyclical *Caritas et Veritate*. He discusses how the environment is a gift to everyone, which does not mean we can do whatever we want, but gives us a responsibility. We need to reject, he says, the "technical dominion over nature, because the natural environment is more than raw material to be manipulated at our pleasure; it is a wondrous work of the Creator containing a 'grammar' which sets forth ends and criteria for its wise use, not its reckless exploitation" (CV 48).

From these kernels of wisdom Pope Francis developed his full encyclical about the environment, *Laudato Si*.' It has the subtitle "Care for our Common Home," so even at its beginning it contains an implicit understanding of the common good. Francis takes up the idea of our disordered relationship with the natural world and devotes an entire section to what he calls the "technocratic paradigm."

Francis defines the technocratic paradigm as one that "exalts the concept of a subject who, using logic and rational procedures, progressively approaches and gains control over an external object" (LS 106). There are many things about a technocratic approach to problems that are good. We use the scientific method to explore the world, ask questions, and learn new things. It helps us build technologies that can improve lives. The problem arises when this paradigm turns the natural world into an object from which we "extract everything possible." The relationship has become "confrontational" rather than relational (LS 106). (Remember Philemon and Onesimus?) Another children's book, *The Giving Tree*, can demonstrate this concept. In this book, a tree gives and gives and gives until it has nothing left. At the same time, a human takes and takes and takes with no concern for the impact of the extraction. When I was a new parent, I would read this book to my kids and think, "wow, that's a great model of a selfless parent." I recently re-read it and I thought, "wow, this is an unhealthy relationship." The technocratic paradigm looks at a tree and asks "what do I need?" It's unhealthy.

Pope Francis points out how many problems in our world today flow from this technocratic paradigm. As an approach to the world, it has become almost "unconscious" in its common assumption. The problem is that while technology masquerades as being neutral, or even positive—"look how this can improve your life"—quite often, the opposite is the case. As Francis claims, "we have to accept that technological products are not neutral, for they create a framework which ends up conditioning lifestyles and shaping social possibilities along the lines dictated by the interests of certain powerful groups" (LS 107).

Let's illustrate this with an example. I suspect that most people today think electric cars are an important part of the solution to pollution. It makes sense: if the cars are polluting the air, let's make them electric and solve the problem. The logic of this approach to pollution illustrates Francis's point perfectly. Electric cars require electricity that has to come from somewhere. An electric car's carbon footprint depends on where you live and how your electricity is generated. Seeing electric cars as a solution to the climate crisis shows our captivity to the technocratic paradigm. It shifts the extraction to different parts of the planet (rare metals) and requires nothing selfless of us at all.

The way corporations advertise electric cars will also help us see how they derive from a technocratic paradigm. Car companies are selling a lifestyle. The cars are lauded as quick, zippy, and hip. They allow you to signal your virtue to the world. These cars are luxurious, quiet, and powerful. These are the exact same things that companies use to sell us cars with internal combustion engines! Here are some advertising tag lines for electric cars that I found using a google image search:

- We don't feel range anxiety. We feel range ambition.
- All out everything.
- Zero emissions. Zero compromises.
- Pure design.
- Upgrade from the middle seat to the driver's seat.
- Silent in a loud world.
- Electrifying.
- Keep the world adventurous forever.

These vehicles are marketed as the latest, the best, the cutting edge of what technology can provide. This is the technocratic paradigm. Electric cars are presented to us as a chance for selfishness. They ask nothing of us. Their sales are fueled (no pun intended) by profit. Our economic concerns overwhelm and take over every advance in technology.

The "green" revolution of electric cars, or other technologies that might help us overcome our environmental crisis, prevents us from seeing the true depth of the problem. "How can we find cleaner cars?" is the wrong question. We need to ask: "Why do we live in a world where a car is necessary?" "Why have we built cities where we have to drive everywhere we go?" "Why are so few cities walkable?" "Why do so few cities have good public transportation?" There is only one answer to these questions: "selfishness." The American ideal of independence, control, and freedom overwhelms any view of the common good. I can think of no idea more opposed to the common good than the calm, powerful, solid, serene image of a human ensconced in leather driving a car across an empty landscape. It is an icon we worship. It takes us in the opposite direction from the common good.

If our efforts at environmentalism are cloaked in "the accumulation of constant novelties" and a "superficiality" grounded in consumerism, then we have already lost. The logic of the market, the logic that tries to sell us stuff and desires profit above all else, cannot be the logic that will break us out of the cycle. We need something more than small shifts in consumer behavior. If we want to live in proper relationship with the world around us, if we want to be able to say with a straight face that we seek the common good, we need a "bold cultural revolution." We need to "slow down and look at reality in a different way . . . to recover the values and the great goals swept away by our unrestrained delusions of grandeur" (LS 114).

The mixture of our "green" economy and a consumerist mindset actually blinds us from having concern for the common good. The technological paradigm, which feeds us an endless string of products—our wants presented as if they were needs—results in acedia, a spiritual deadness. A paradigm of technological solutions and consumerism "leads people to believe that they are free as long as they have the supposed freedom to consume" (LS 203). The sad irony is, however, that it's really the companies and corporations who are in control. Our freedom of choice leads to no freedom at all.[8] Francis says this much better than I can:

> When people become self-centered and self-enclosed, their greed increases. The emptier a person's heart is, the more he or she needs things to buy, own and consume. It becomes almost impossible to accept the limits imposed by reality. In this horizon, a genuine sense of the common good also disappears. . . . Obsession with a consumerist lifestyle, above all when few people are capable of maintaining it, can only lead to violence and mutual destruction. (LS 204)

Ultimately, what is called for to achieve the common good, both in terms of ecology and more broadly in society, is personal transformation: "Many things have to change course, but it is we human beings above all who need to change" (LS 202). These changes can't be small. Nor can they flow from the logic of consumerism or selfishness. They need to be self-sacrificial. They need, like Philemon, to result in the crumbling of our world. If we make them, we will, like Jeremiah, be viewed as outcasts. We must let God's grace dismantle our facile desires and need for control.

We must, at every turn, make the self-sacrificial choice. If and when we fail, we need to be resolute in working to make a better choice at the next opportunity. We must live justly for others. The only way to achieve this is by going out from ourselves and seeking encounter with the other, just as Jesus himself did. More Francis:

> We are always capable of going out of ourselves towards the other. Unless we do this, other creatures will not be recognized for their true worth; we are unconcerned about caring for things for the sake of others; we fail to set limits on ourselves in order to avoid the suffering of others or the deterioration of our surroundings. Disinterested concern for others, and the rejection of every form of self-centeredness and self-absorption, are essential if we truly wish to care for our brothers and sisters and for the natural environment. These attitudes also attune us to the moral imperative

---

8. See William T. Cavanaugh, *Being Consumed: Economics and Christian Desire* (Grand Rapids, MI: Eerdmans, 2008), particularly chapter 1, "Freedom and Unfreedom."

of assessing the impact of our every action and personal decision on the world around us. If we can overcome individualism, we will truly be able to develop a different lifestyle and bring about significant changes in society. (LS 208)

In other words: Be transformed.

Conclusion

Attending to Transformation

A star looks down at me,
And says: "Here I and you
Stand each in our degree:
What do you mean to do,—
　　Mean to do?"

I say: "For all I know,
Wait, and let Time go by,
Till my change come."—"Just so,"
The star says: "So mean I:—
　　So mean I."

　　　　　　　　　　—Thomas Hardy

This poem, titled "Waiting Both," can help us think about transformation. How do we change? What is transformation's catalyst? Where and how does it begin?

According to Hardy's poem, change comes by waiting. If a star has enough time, its chemical reactions will result in dramatic change. The same is true for humans, Hardy says: wait, let time go by, and change will come. There is wisdom in Hardy's poem. We all change across time. Sometimes we change slowly (I think, for example, of my hairline). We also sometimes change in an instant. An unexpected death, a cancer diagnosis, the birth of a child, a new love—these sudden changes come to us unbidden. Humans, Hardy suggests, slip through time waiting for our change to come, instigated by forces beyond our control.

Hardy's view, however, is not particularly Christian. Believers are not left to the vagaries of life and the passing of time. We believe that God shapes us and transforms us.

We also have agency in our own change. As Christians, we can *attend* to our own transformation. As the philosopher Simone Weil writes, "if we turn our minds toward the good, it is impossible that little by little the whole soul will not be attracted thereto in spite of itself."[1] She means that attending to spiritual matters will shape our soul toward proper ends. We are not, like the star in Hardy's poem, left to the passing of time, hoping that our change will come. We can actively help engage and activate our own transformation. In what follows, I'd like to focus on two ways we can attend to our own transformation: prayer and sacrament.

Prayer and Transformation

I am terrible at praying. Maybe I'll blame my upbringing. I grew up in a Protestant Evangelical context in which long, extemporaneous prayers were the order of the day. These prayers were always quite personal and specific, a laundry list of requests. I never felt comfortable with this type of prayer, and to this day I struggle to pray my own words.

When I was a sophomore in college, I studied in Athens, Istanbul, and Rome. This was a culturally and theologically jarring experience. The prayer of Orthodox Christians, Muslims, and Roman Catholics bore no resemblance to the prayer with which I was familiar. I thought praying was about God; we needed the right words and fervency so that God would grant our requests. Then, over several dinners in Athens, Sr. Emmanuel Renner helped me think about prayer differently. I'll never forget when she said to me, "Prayer is for your change, not God's." I almost choked on my souvlaki. She patiently explained to me that prayer is about transformation. It is a way of attending to the kind of person we should aspire to be.

---

1. Simone Weil, "Attention and Will," in *Simone Weil: An Anthology*, ed. Sian Miles (New York: Grove Press, 1986), 212.

This was a "eureka" moment for me. It's one thing to make very specific requests of God, to ask for healing, for help passing a test, or for safety. (And there certainly is a place for this type of intercessory prayer.) It is a very different thing to ask God for peace, for God's presence in our lives, or for courage. If the things we've discussed in this book matter to us, if we care about the poor, about the environment, and those in prison, then prayer must be at the heart of our endeavors. We need to pray for God to create a more just world. We also need to pray for God to transform us into agents of that justice.

The best Christian prayer of transformation is hiding in plain sight. The Lord's Prayer, taken from Matthew 6:9-13, calls for a transformed life. How often, however, do we stop to contemplate its meaning?

Your Kingdom Come . . .

What does it mean to pray for the coming of God's kingdom? We have seen throughout this book that an authentically Christian life, one that is lived in accordance with Scripture and tradition, must not focus only on heaven. We also have a grave obligation to care about this present world. It is important that we pray for God's kingdom because it forces us to think about how different God's kingdom is from the one we want for ourselves. Praying the word *kingdom* suggests that the world we live in is contested space. If God's kingdom needs to come, then there must be some other kingdom it will displace. Human structures of greed and accumulation are inimical to the aims of God.

The *Catechism* makes a similar point, saying that Christians live in the space in-between the current world and the world to come: our "vocation to eternal life does not suppress, but actually reinforces, [our] duty to put into action in this world the energies and means received from the Creator to serve justice and peace" (CCC 2820). Praying for God's kingdom means we must work for a world that is in accordance with the beatitudes (CCC 2821).

Your Will Be Done . . .

The phrase "your will be done" is pregnant with possibilities. At a certain level, it requires of us a dispassionate willingness to stop trying to control our own destinies. We must surrender to God's will. On the other hand, God's will is not a mystery. Scripture and tradition are quite clear about those things which God wills. We see God's will from the beginning of Genesis, when God created humans in God's image and called all to greatness. We see God's will in the prophets, where God wanted a society with justice for all peoples. We see God's will in Paul's letters, which call for enshrining the weak at the center of the body of Christ. We see God's will in the gospels, when Jesus says that feeding the hungry is the same thing as feeding him. We see God's will when St. Basil says that our extra possessions belong to the poor. We see God's will throughout Catholic social teaching, which calls for a world of solidarity and freedom so that all of God's creation can flourish. God's will, it turns out, is well established.

The Lord's Prayer testifies that the peace, harmony, and love that we know exists in heaven sets the standard for the work we need to do in this world. An informed reading of this prayer should make us gasp at the broad agenda it sets for us to accomplish, with God's help. When we pray "thy kingdom come, thy will be done," we commit ourselves to a transformed life that works to transform the world.

Give Us This Day Our Daily Bread . . .

The only concrete request in the Lord's prayer is for "our daily bread." It provides no language for anything beyond what our daily needs require. It does not ask for security for tomorrow. It does not create space for 401k or 403b retirement accounts. It simply asks for daily food. We can hear in this request an echo of the church's teaching about the universal destination of goods. The goods of the earth are not ours to accumulate beyond our immediate needs.

We also should see "our daily bread" as a reference to the Lord's Supper (especially when we recite it during the Liturgy of the Eucharist). We seek the bread of life that only God can provide in this sacred meal. It is daily sustenance for our life of faith.

For those of us who do not face literal hunger on a daily basis, however, the prayer for daily bread calls us to "exercise responsibility" toward those who are hungry "in solidarity with the human family" (CCC 2831). A spiritual focus should not cloud our vision from the "drama of hunger in the world" (CCC 2831). Informed by the parable of the poor man and Lazarus, by Matthew 25, and by the profile of justice in a prophet like Amos, we can see that praying for daily bread sets a real-world task for the one who prays sincerely. Pope Benedict also points out this connection between the prayer and the physical needs of the hungry: "The prayer which we repeat at every Mass: 'Give us this day our daily bread,' obliges us to do everything possible . . . to end or at least reduce the scandal of hunger and malnutrition afflicting so many millions of people in our world, especially developing countries" (SC 91).[2]

Our Father . . .

Finally, we should note that the language in the Lord's prayer is communal. The first Greek words are in the first-person plural—"*Our Father.*" The prayer's mention of daily bread, forgiveness, and deliverance are all collective and communal. This is not *my* father or *your* father, but all of ours collectively. God's collective parenthood means that we are all sisters and brothers, that we belong to each other. Thus, the language of the prayer compels us to think about something beyond our individual selves and to think about being in solidarity with others. In this we find an echo of the church's teaching on the common good. All lives ought to be oriented toward the collective in order to build a sense of belonging to one human family. We should always choose the good of the other over our own good.

Prayer Is about Us

Prayer is addressed to God, but it is mostly about us. If our attitude toward prayer is that we're hoping to get something from God, then we've missed the point. The Lord's Prayer provides a model of what prayer should be like. It makes very few specific requests of God beyond daily sustenance. It provides a model of reciprocal forgiveness, which expresses how humans need to be in a proper relationship with one another. And it asks that our cosmic destiny be shepherded by God, not the evil one.

2. Pope Benedict XVI, *Sacramentum Caritatis*, February 22, 2007, https://www.vatican.va/content/benedict-xvi/en/apost_exhortations/documents/hf_ben-xvi_exh_20070222_sacramentum-caritatis.html.

There is an ethical demand within the Lord's Prayer. Once we look closely at it, we find a call for the community of believers to have an outward, selfless disposition. It demands that we submit to God's will, limit our accumulations, and focus on others before ourselves. In brief, the prayer asks us to be transformed into agents of love and mercy for the world around us.

Eucharist and Transformation

How many times have you heard the Eucharist referred to as the "source and summit" of our faith as Catholics? I hear it constantly, and for good reason. This phrase, which originates with the Second Vatican Council's *Lumen Gentium*, attempts to encapsulate the way in which the "Church draws her life from the Eucharist" (EE 1).[3]

My frustration with this phrase is that I rarely hear anyone explain what it means. What does it mean to call the Eucharist our source and summit? On one hand, there are probably hundreds of ways to unpack that phrase; it might mean something slightly different to everyone. We all walk our own journey of faith, and the Eucharist might mean something unique to each of us.

I do get concerned, however, when the phrase "source and summit" gets used as if its meaning is fully clear. In particular, this phrase often goes hand in hand with a certain type of personal eucharistic piety. I often hear it used to advocate for eucharistic adoration and the need to come to Mass. While the Eucharist should be adored and Mass is essential, these things do not exhaust the church's teaching on the Eucharist. For the church fully to draw her life from the Eucharist as our "source and summit," we must also think about how it relates to our actions in the world.

To help explain this, I turn first to the encyclical *Ecclesia de Eucharistia*, written by Pope John Paul II in 2003. John Paul notes that any understanding of the Eucharist that does not apply itself to making a more just world is insufficient. He notes how dark our world is, with poverty, injustice, and war, a "world where the weakest, the most

---

3. Pope John Paul II, *Ecclesia de Eucharistia*, April 17, 2003, https://www.vatican.va/holy_father/special_features/encyclicals/documents/hf_jp-ii_enc_20030417_ecclesia_eucharistia_en.html.

powerless and the poorest appear to have so little hope!" In precisely this context a eucharistic hope is needed:

> For this reason too, the Lord wished to remain with us in the Eucharist, making his presence in meal and sacrifice the promise of a humanity renewed by his love. . . . Proclaiming the death of the Lord "until he comes" (1 Cor 11:26) entails that all who take part in the Eucharist be committed to changing their lives and making them in a certain way completely "Eucharistic." [This] is this fruit of a transfigured existence and a commitment to transforming the world in accordance with the Gospel. (EE 20)

In other words, if we are a Eucharistic people, we must be transformed in such a way that our lives transform the world. As we will see below, this idea is embedded in Scripture from our very earliest glimpses of the Christian practice of the Lord's Supper.

Eucharist in Corinth

Paul was worried when he left Corinth in the middle of the first century. They were an unruly bunch, in an unruly town, and he wasn't sure exactly how well they would be able to hold true to the things he had taught them. His fledgling church, meeting in several homes throughout ancient Corinth, had to learn to walk on its own. Paul was needed elsewhere.

It didn't take long for the rumors to spread. Eventually Paul received confirmation from a trusted delegation that the church in Corinth was splintering. There were many issues dividing them: speaking in tongues; food sacrificed to idols; sexual immorality; and, most shockingly, the Eucharist itself. When the church was gathering for the Lord's Supper, rich people were eating lavish meals in front of everyone, while the poor had nothing.

Paul reminds them of the words of institution that he received (words we still hear at every Mass). Then, he says, "Whoever, therefore, eats the bread or drinks the cup of the Lord in an unworthy manner will be answerable for the body and blood of the Lord" (1 Cor 11:27). The Corinthians need to examine themselves before they eat or drink. And then he adds, "For all who eat and drink without discerning the body, eat and drink judgment against themselves" (v. 29).

When Paul says to "discern the body," he means that Christians need to think about the whole. There are many parts but there is just one body. Each member has its role to play and should not think too highly of itself. For Paul, the one who is unworthy to partake of the Lord's Supper is the one who puts his or her own rights before those of another. Pride, greed, arrogance, or selfishness would make one unworthy.

Paul then takes his understanding of the Eucharist even farther: "the members of the body that seem to be weaker are indispensable, and those members of the body that we think less honorable we clothe with greater honor, and our less respectable members are treated with greater respect" (1 Cor 12:22-23). The weak need to be enshrined at the center. It's not just that they should be admitted, but they need to be integrated, given the place of honor.

In our earliest glimpse of the Christian community gathered around the table, there are problems. Paul focuses attention on the meaning of the Eucharist and the need to discern its proper implications. The Eucharist not only unites us but should compel us to put others before ourselves: "God has so arranged the body, giving the greater honor to the inferior member, that there may be no dissension within the body" (1 Cor 12:24-25). The Eucharist compels us to selfless integration. In an ironic way, for Paul, integrating the weak will make the body stronger.

Eucharist in John's Gospel

We have four gospels in the New Testament because each of their authors wanted to offer a unique interpretation of Jesus' life and its meaning (see Luke 1:1-4). Three of our gospels, Matthew, Mark, and Luke, are similar to each other; we call these three the Synoptic Gospels. The Gospel of John, however, is unique. In fact, John was a bit of a maverick.[4] John knew of Paul and his letters. He knew about the Lord's Supper and the words Jesus spoke to his disciples at the Passover. Yet, when he sits down to write his story, John leaves them out. You can read the whole gospel; they're not in there! John wants his readers to think about the meaning of the Eucharist, beyond its words of institution.

---

4. I borrow this language from Robert Kysar, *John, the Maverick Gospel*, 3rd ed. (Philadelphia: Westminster/John Knox Press, 2007).

The thirteenth chapter of John introduces the Passover. The disciples, just like in the other gospels, gather to eat the meal together. This is where John the maverick strikes. He removes the familiar language of institution, "this is my body," and narrates a story that is only in his gospel. Jesus "got up from the table, took off his outer robe, and tied a towel around himself" (13:4). Jesus proceeds to wash his disciples' feet, pointing directly to the importance of his example:

> Do you know what I have done to you? You call me Teacher and Lord—and you are right, for that is what I am. So if I, your Lord and Teacher, have washed your feet, you also ought to wash one another's feet. For I have set you an example, that you also should do as I have done to you. (John 13:12-15)

The maverick's message here is not too hard to figure out. The Lord's Supper is about service. The Eucharist is about what we do for each other, modeled on what the Lord has done for us.

Earlier in John, Jesus says "the bread that I will give for the life of the world is my flesh" (John 6:51). Catholics point to such language as foundational for our understanding of Christ's real presence in the Eucharist. Note, however, that the Lord's flesh is "for the life of the world." The real presence is about more than spiritual life. Jesus' concrete act of service in the foot washing tells us as much. "For the life of the world" refers to our spiritual life *and* our need to commit ourselves to concrete service in the world. John Paul II emphasizes the way the Gospel of John brings out the "profound meaning" of the Eucharist, "in which Jesus appears as the teacher of communion and service" (EE 20).

Pope Benedict, in his exhortation *Sacramentum Caritatis*, focuses the third of its three major sections on how the Eucharist is a mystery to be offered to the world. Here he leaves no doubt about the clear connection between mission and the Eucharist:

> Our communities, when they celebrate the Eucharist, must become ever more conscious that the sacrifice of Christ is for all, and that the Eucharist thus compels all who believe in him to become "bread that is broken" for others, to work for the building of a more just and fraternal world. (SC 88)

Take this quotation, or at least the idea within it, to your parishes and ask: how well are we doing? Are we finding ways to help our Eucharistic piety be both personal and social? How do we help people live out the grace and mercy that we ourselves have received? Do we help people understand that the "source and summit" of our faith entails both spiritual food and literal food?

When I look back across the content and concepts in the five chapters of this book—covering the various social teachings and their biblical roots—there is a way in which they all cohere in the end. They all, in various ways, call for transformation. The Eucharist is a transformation; the host changes and becomes the Lord's body and blood. This is more than a mystery to be contemplated, but also empowers in us the same transformation. The real presence then resides in three places at once: in the host, in the poor whom we experience, and in ourselves, enlivened and empowered by the sacrament to be bread that is broken for the world.

Sacrifice

Humans have always lived in the breach between the world that exists and the world for which we long. This breach is also evident in our very selves. We struggle to live out and live up to the process of being transformed into the self-sacrificial way of the cross. The artistic image on the cover of this book demonstrates this tension very well. The well-known scene of the transfiguration sets for us the ideal, a glimpse of Jesus' true identity. The disciples, cowering toward the bottom, struggle to understand. This image, however, is refracted and pixelated. We cannot see the full path of our transformed life since our vision is veiled by our imperfections and sin. St. Paul feels this deeply. All of creation, he says, is groaning with labor pains; we all seek the liberation that only God can bring (Rom 8:18-22). The call to "be transformed" is more of a process than a point of arrival. We all live in the process of becoming.

The title for this book, *Be Transformed*, comes from Paul's letter to the Romans (12:2). In the preceding verse, Paul says, "present your bodies as a living sacrifice, holy and acceptable to God, which is your spiritual worship" (Rom 12:1). Transformation requires sacrifice. Whether talking about structural sin, solidarity, the universal destination of goods, the preferential option for the poor, or the common good, the starting point to achieve all these goals, and the thing which binds them all together, is sacrifice.

Sacrifice that leads to transformation, as I've noted consistently throughout this book, will not find a comfortable home in our world. Everything about a sacrificial way of living will seem unfair. A transformed life will clash with what the world tells us our life should be like. A Christian should not find him or herself comfortable in the world because "the world is a dangerous place for the elect."[5] Or at least it should be.

I can't think of a better way to end this book than with the opening lines of *Gaudium et Spes*, the pastoral constitution from Vatican II about the place of the church in the modern world:

> The joys and the hopes, the griefs and the anxieties of the [people] of this age, especially those who are poor or in any way afflicted, these too are the joys and hopes, the cries and the anxieties of the followers of Christ. (GS 1)

With this sentence as our star, we must embark like the magi to a destination unknown, our only assurance God's presence and grace, transformation of self and world our calling.

---

5. Donald H. Juel, *Mark* (Minneapolis: Fortress Press, 1990), 186.

Subject Index

Scripture Index

About the Cover

The art featured on the front and back covers of the print edition of this book are icons painted by Kelly Latimore. According to the artist, *Glitch Transfiguration*, which is featured on the front, was created with his nephew by "happy accident." The original piece, *The Transfiguration* is inset on the back cover. As Latimore states on his website, "The light we think we hold has already been reflecting and scattering in all directions . . ."